Nourishing the Spirit

Nourishing the Spirit

The Healing Emotions of Wonder, Joy, Compassion and Hope

JAMES D. WHITEHEAD

AND

EVELYN EATON WHITEHEAD

ORBIS BOOKS

Maryknoll, New York 10545

Founded in 1970, Orbis Books endeavors to publish works that enlighten the mind, nourish the spirit, and challenge the conscience. The publishing arm of the Maryknoll Fathers and Brothers, Orbis seeks to explore the global dimensions of the Christian faith and mission, to invite dialogue with diverse cultures and religious traditions, and to serve the cause of reconciliation and peace. The books published reflect the views of their authors and do not represent the official position of the Maryknoll Society. To learn more about Maryknoll and Orbis Books, please visit our website at www.maryknollsociety.org.

Published by Orbis Books, Maryknoll, New York 10545-0302.
Manufactured in the United States of America.
Manuscript editing and typesetting by Joan Weber Laflamme.

Library of Congress Cataloging-in-Publication Data

Whitehead, James D.
  Nourishing the spirit : the healing emotions of wonder, joy, compassion, and hope / James D. Whitehead and Evelyn Eaton Whitehead.
      p. cm.
  ISBN 978-1-62698-001-3 (pbk.)
  1. Spiritual life—Catholic Church. 2. Emotions—Religious aspects—Catholic Church. 3. Christianity—Psychology. 4. Positive psychology. I. Whitehead, Evelyn Eaton. II. Title.
  BX2350.3.W47 2012
  248.4—dc23
                                                                                    2012007390

with thanks,
for simple feasts and friendship

Toots and Bill Foy   Judy and Ed Logue
Patricia Hackett and Rita Koehler   Eleanor and Bob Roemer

Contents

Prologue: Blessed and Broken   ix

Part I
Moral Emotions

1. Emotions in the Life of Faith   3

2. Wonder, Awe and Reverence   13

3. The Rehabilitation of Emotion   23

4. Anger, Courage and Hope   33

5. Curiosity and Contentment   43

Part II
Healing Emotions

6. Joy and Happiness   55

7. Transformations of Love   65

8. Virtues of Pride and Humility   77

9. Compassion and Self-Care   87

10. Mood Swings in the Life of Faith   97

Part III
Religious Emotions

11. Ennobling Passions—Faith, Hope and Charity   109

12. Gratitude and Generosity   119

13. The Works of Justice and Mercy   127

14. Emotions in Spiritual Transformation   137

15. Religion and Ways of Knowing   147

Additional Resources   157

The Vocabulary of Healing Emotions   167

Bibliography   169

Index   177

Prologue

Blessed and Broken

We recognize ourselves as both blessed and broken. Each of us has received innumerable gifts—of life, nurture, companionship, forgiveness. And each of us bears scars that both record and cover over our brokenness—injuries self-inflicted and inherited; mistakes, blunders, and offenses; losses we continue to mourn.

This image of blessed and broken originates for Christians in the story of Jesus' life. At his final meal with friends he is remembered to have taken up bread, blessed and broken it to share with them. The next day his own body, blessed by God, was broken on a cross. In the larger Christian story this paradox describes every life, with its journey marked by both gratitude and grief.

Our lives as broken call forth a range of emotions—sorrow, grief, guilt—and the more complex virtues of compassion and forgiveness that bind up shattered hearts and bruised psyches.

Our lives as blessed frame the many positive emotions—joy, delight, wonder, pride—as well as the more complex dispositions—attachment, contentment, gratitude—that enrich our lives. These rich resources witness to the sage judgment of Bishop Irenaeus in the second century that "the glory of God is the human person fully alive."

In the chapters ahead we explore the positive emotions as they perform two paradoxical operations: feelings of joy and contentment usher us into a deeper awareness and comfort with ourselves; emotions of appreciation and awe lift us out of ourselves in ways that expand and enrich us.

Every life is shaped by these dual impulses—to become more attentive to our own interior life, with all its graces and ghost; and to become more attuned to what lies beyond us: the lives of loved ones, the needs of the world, the healing presence of a mysterious God.

Part I

MORAL EMOTIONS

Christian life is a story of powerful emotions—joy and thanksgiving, regret and sorrow, courage and hope.

Our religious ancestors in Israel leveraged every powerful feeling, whether consoling or disturbing, into a deepening relationship with their mysterious God.

The rehabilitation of emotion—both in the social sciences and in spirituality—invites us to embrace anew the moral emotions that serve as guides to a flourishing life of grace.

Our exploration begins with the emotions of wonder and awe, movements that serve as portals to religious experience.

The story of faith includes the virtue of courage, with its complements of tempered anger, tamed fear and the surprising energy of hope.

Part I concludes with a reflection on the emotional trajectory that moves us from curiosity to appreciation and often, to an abiding mood of contentment.

1

Emotions in the Life of Faith

Spirituality reflects humanity's biological press for connection and community building as much as it reflects the individual's need for sacred revelation.

—PSYCHIATRIST GEORGE VAILLANT

The life of faith is a passionate affair. Beloved by God, we respond with affection and care toward our loved ones and those in need. We are aroused by injustice, moved by generosity, awed by the stunning beauty of the world. Despite life's setbacks and reversals of fortune, passionate hope sustains us.

Embracing these emotions, we take our lead from the scriptures. A cornucopia of feelings pours out in the psalms; emotions—positive and painful—burst forth without apology or restraint. Psalm 1 proclaims: "Happy are those who do not follow the advice of the wicked." And throughout this biblical poetry sentiments of gladness, delight and rejoicing resound. "You show me the path of life. In your presence there is fullness of joy. In your right hand are pleasures evermore" (Ps 16). Negative emotions, too, arise without ceasing: "I am weary with my moaning . . . my eyes are wasted away with grief" (Ps 7).

The Book of Psalms is a storehouse of intense emotion. Our Hebrew ancestors were utterly at home with these forceful feelings. Every movement of the heart, however painful or pleasurable, turned them toward Yahweh. "Clap your hands, all you peoples; shout to God with loud songs of joy for the Lord, the Most High, is awesome" (Ps 47). This expanse of feelings chronicled their deepening relationship with a mysterious God.

The first generations of Christians, mindful of their spiritual heritage rooted in Jewish thought, were strongly influenced by another cultural interpretation of emotion. Stoic philosophy, dominant then throughout the Greek-speaking world, argued that achieving the ideal of tranquility required extinguishing all movements of passion. Christians became tempted to replace the gospel images of Jesus being moved by strong emotions—anger, sadness, fear—with a more sedate vision: Jesus as "meek and humble of heart" (Mt 11:29). In the understandings of the life of faith that developed in these early centuries in the West, this overly cautious approach to emotions began to win out.

So Christians, urged to disengage themselves from volatile passions, sometimes settled into complacent routines and dispassionate moods. Negative emotions of fear (of possibly doing wrong) and guilt (of having done wrong) came to dominate their emotional life. Caution displaced courage; composure warned against the risk of adventures. The passion of anger was declared one of the seven deadly sins, disqualifying its contribution in our response to malice and injustice. Exuberant celebration was discouraged in the interest of sobriety and good order. Such a becalmed mood gave muted witness to the "good news of our salvation."

Today many within and beyond the community of faith are exploring links between powerful emotions and the spiritual quest. This contemporary interest reclaims an insight championed by Thomas Aquinas in the thirteenth century. Drawing on the Greek philosopher Aristotle, Aquinas made a compelling case for the link between virtue and passion. In a radical departure from the dominant piety of his time, Aquinas insisted that "moral virtues cannot be without the passions." For Aquinas, virtue and strong emotion are not adversaries. Love and courage and devotion are passions, now become virtues.

The Contribution of Positive Psychology

The psalms testify that our emotions play a role on the spiritual journey. The psychological disciplines today offer additional insight into the complex dynamics of our emotional lives. Early in its development the science of psychology focused attention on illness and dysfunction. Sigmund Freud and other early practitioners sought methods of analysis and cure, hoping to relieve the suffering of their patients. In this initial season, then, psychology sought a remedial goal.

As president of the American Psychology Association in 1997, Martin Seligman argued for expanding the scope of research and practice to include a commitment to *positive psychology*. This shift would establish human flourishing as a central concern of psychological inquiry, effecting "a change of focus from repairing what is worst in life to creating what is best" and developing "a science of personal strength, or of social responsibility, or of human virtue."

Psychologist Daniel Siegel describes the benefits of this approach: "Positive psychology has offered an important corrective to the disease model by identifying the characteristics of happy people, such as gratitude, compassion, open-mindedness, and curiosity." In the chapters ahead we draw on the findings of positive psychology for additional insight into the role of emotions in the spiritual journey today.

Emotions Painful and Positive

The *painful emotions* of anger, fear and anxiety support our survival; the *healing emotions* of love, appreciation and compassion help us thrive. Negative emotions arise in defense of our life and dignity. Positive emotions celebrate our life and dignity. Negative emotions narrow our focus as we confront significant dangers and threats. Positive emotions broaden our focus as we savor the goodness of creation. Painful emotions, in the service of survival, deplete our energy reserves and quickly exhaust us. Positive emotions, in service of our well-being, renew our energy even as they give rest to our spirit.

The distressing emotions of anger, fear, sadness, and grief train our attention on immediate dangers by activating the sympathetic nervous system. This physiological network—an essential part of the wisdom of the body—readies us to deal with threat by increasing heart rate, blood pressure and cardiac output. The nervous system activated by these painful arousals shuts down the digestive system and sends fatty acids into the bloodstream, providing quick energy to the body, preparing us for fight or flight.

These painful emotions, then, are essential dynamics in a meaningful life. But their arousals are both expensive and volatile. Expensive because they rapidly consume our energy, depleting our resources and leaving us feeling exhausted; volatile as they escalate into chronic moods and evoke toxic behavior. Anger, defender of our dignity, mushrooms into chronic resentment. Fear's early warning system spirals into a paralyzing phobia. Guilt, meant as a guardian of our goodness, twists into a cruel judge of every action or impulse. When these essential emotions spread beyond their proper domains, they darken our world, casting shadows over experiences of joy, delight and appreciation. Burdened by painful emotions that have become chronic, we have little energy available for empathy or hope or even curiosity.

Positive emotions—joy, compassion, pride—often have to elbow their way into our schedules, claiming space that had been ceded to all-consuming negative affects. These healing emotions activate the parasympathetic nervous system, helping us relax even as energy is restored. In opposition to the sympathetic nervous system more closely linked to negative emotions, here the wisdom of the body lowers metabolism, respiratory rate and muscle tension. The nerves that activate these positive feelings decrease heart rate and blood pressure, facilitating digestion and stimulating circulation. Psychiatrist George Vaillant distinguishes these two essential resources: "The sympathetic nervous system is catabolic: fight-or-flight uses up the body's resources. The parasympathetic nervous system is anabolic: faith, hope, and cuddling build up the body's resources." And, he adds, "While pain, rage, and grief provide short term benefits, positive emotions provide benefits over the long term."

Confirming Vaillant's position, psychologists note an important difference in the actions engendered. Both positive and painful emotions equip us to respond. The adrenaline rush of fear and anger fuels forceful responses of self-defense. But healing emotions, such as contentment and appreciation, evoke the gentler response of a calming mood. Serotonin and dopamine, markers of our positive emotional states, play more important roles here.

The Healing Emotions

At first the phrase *healing emotions* may remind us of our own painful feelings that still await healing: repeated surges of anger, or overwhelming grief, or debilitating fear. But the emotions we examine here—gratitude, mercy, wonder, hope—represent healing in another sense. These arousals promote the healing of the heart.

Gratitude heals amnesia—our careless forgetfulness of the bounty that daily surrounds us. Feeling grateful, we are reminded of favors freely given, of benefits received. This emotion challenges our sense of entitlement, with its miserly focus on calculating what we deserve.

The emotion of mercy heals wounds accumulated by miscarriages of justice and softens the harshness of justice unrelieved. Mercy reaches out in compassion, inviting us—as James Keenan writes—"to enter into the chaos of another." Mercy heals what justice cannot correct.

The emotion of wonder, drawing us out of our usual self-absorption, opens us to the splendor of the world around us. Feelings of awe move us toward respect and reverence; we are confronted by realities not ordered to our own narrow purposes. These hints of transcendence leave us comforted and healed.

The emotion of hope frees us from the jaded sense that nothing ever really changes, from the weary conviction that the future will hold only more of the same. Hope honors openness to the future, as proclaimed by the prophet Isaiah: "Behold I am doing something new. Now it breaks forth. Do you not perceive it?"

In these examples and others we examine in the chapters ahead, emotions bind up and heal our vulnerable lives. Psychologists discuss this healing quality in terms of the positive emotions' capacity to *broaden and build* our resources.

Broaden and Build

Psychologist Barbara Fredrickson has pioneered the study of the expansive effects of the healing emotions. In contrast to negative emotions, which narrow our attention on immediate action meant to overcome present threat, positive emotions broaden and build our adaptive capacity. These emotions expand the options available to us—both by widening our awareness of the situation at hand and by generating new possibilities for action. In Frederickson's words, "These broadened mindsets carry indirect and long-term adaptive benefits, because broadening also builds enduring personal resources which function as reserves to be drawn on later."

Love strengthens our links with those who are close to us; affection connects us with those eager to support our well-being and ready to rally to our assistance. And the feelings are mutual! The emotion of appreciation enriches our recognition of the beauty and goodness that already surround us. Compassion builds bridges between us and those who are in distress. The mood of contentment creates a comfort zone in which we build on and integrate the many blessings that have come our way.

Fredrickson adds that these gains are more than momentary. Negative emotions seem designed to be intense but transient: once we are alerted to the anger-provoking or fear-inducing threat, these emotions have done their work. As we respond to these alerts, the impact of these painful feelings tends to diminish quickly.

A different rhythm accompanies positive emotions. "The personal resources accrued during states of positive emotions are conceptualized as durable. They outlast the transient emotional states that led to their acquisition." So positive emotions have *staying power.* Even after the feelings fade, an increased sense of personal resourcefulness and self-confidence continues. Feelings of enjoyment linger in a mood of relief and satisfaction. And feelings of hope carry us into the future, expanding our willingness to take risks.

Positive emotions bring additional advantages. The resources released in appreciation and delight not only benefit the future, but they may be able to overcome or correct some of the lingering effects of negative emotions in our past. Fredrickson refers to this possibility as the "undoing hypothesis." As a healthy sense of pride at our achievements brings consolation, it may also serve to decrease a negative residue of earlier shame or an abiding sense of inferiority. As feelings of gratitude take up residence in our heart, our tendency toward jealousy and resentment may be reversed.

Painful emotions contract our vision by focusing attention on present threat. Healing emotions trigger physiological and cognitive changes that "enlarge the field of our peripheral vision," offering a wider perspective. Experiences of wonder and beauty, for example, open our hearts and minds to more of the world around us.

Positive emotions help us adapt to changing circumstances, making us more resilient. With resources of hope and confidence more regularly available, the fallout from life's challenges and setbacks is diminished. We are able to place such events in a broader context, lessening their impact now as well as dispelling any lingering aftereffects.

Susan Neiman includes reverence among the emotions that broaden and build. "Reverence contains admiration as well as gratitude," she notes. When we give attention to what we *revere*, we recover our own rightful place in the world. We remember that we are recipients of marvels and mysteries amid the pains and losses that also populate the environment. The beneficial disorientation brought about by wonder and awe reorients our world. In this refreshing posture we more easily turn away from taking ourselves too seriously, demanding our "rights," and insisting on imagined privileges. "These are feelings that enlarge us," Neiman insists, "and make us better than before."

Mapping Emotional Domains

In his important work *The Compassionate Mind,* Paul Gilbert identifies three distinguishable emotion regulation systems in the brain: (1) an excitement and goal-seeking system; (2) a threat protection system; and (3) a calming system. This schema provides a more nuanced picture of emotions than a simple negative/positive emotion distinction.

The goal-seeking system energizes us to pursue our needs, wants and desires. "This system motivates and directs us to important resources.

GOAL SEEKING
Arousals (desire, hope, longing)
designed to energize our search for
resources we are in need of.

*"My body aches for you, O Lord
like a dry and weary land."*
(Psalm 63)

PROTECTING
Painful stirrings (anger, anxiety,
fear) that alert us to danger and
would defend us from harm.

*"But Jesus perceived their malice, and said,
'Why are you testing me, you hypocrites?'*
(Matthew 22:12)

CALMING
Soothing emotions (joy, affection,
contentment) designed to restore calm
and support a sense of well-being.

*"Peace I leave with you, my peace I give unto you...
let not your heart be troubled, neither let it be afraid."*
(John 14:27)

Adapted from Paul Gilbert, *The Compassionate Mind.*

It is a source of anticipation and pleasure. It underpins the development of desires and some goals—both material goals and those linked to self-esteem." The function of this system is to seek out necessary resources; it is *a system of desires* that guides us toward important life goals. Dopamine is the hormone most associated with the goal-seeking emotions of the drive system.

The threat-protecting system is rooted in the most ancient areas of the brain. Humans are wired to protect ourselves in the face of danger, and the emotions of anger, anxiety and fear are especially focused on this task. Gilbert comments: "Its function is to notice threats quickly through attention-focusing . . . and then give us bursts of feeling such as anxiety, anger or disgust. These feelings ripple through our bodies, alerting and urging us to take action to do something about the threat."

This physiological system operates as each person's department of defense. Dedicated to our survival, this system puts the body on alert—increasing heart rate, blood pressure and cardiac output. As the stress hormones cortisol and adrenaline are released, these emotions narrow our cognitive focus, drawing our full attention to the immediate dangers at hand. When this regulation system becomes unbalanced, destructive behaviors (rage, phobia, cowardly retreat) result.

The threat-protecting system of emotions often defends the goal-seeking emotions. We act spontaneously to help a person who has fallen in the street. Compassion moves us in this generous intent. As we approach the scene a stranger advances, intent on robbing the fallen man. Now our anger and fear are aroused. We will need this energy—and the courage it provokes—to complete the act of compassion.

The calming or contentment system triggers feelings and moods of well-being (joy, appreciation, gratitude, contentment). Gilbert describes this as "a specialized affect regulation system that underpins feelings of reassurance, safeness and well-being." The neurotransmitters serotonin and oxytocin, associated with empathy and caring behavior, are especially active in the calming system. Serotonin helps smooth out anxiety, depression and mood fluctuations; oxytocin is released when we feel close and connected to others. Caring for one's children, ministering to the grief-stricken, and sensitive care for those in need all depend on this system to settle jangled nerves and anxious emotions.

The calming system works in two ways. A period of strenuous goal-seeking often concludes, quite naturally, in a mood of contentment. Hours spent focused on a challenging task give way to an evening of satisfying relaxation. Or a week of stressful attention to a work project finally ends in a weekend given over to relief and rest.

Yet for many of our contemporaries, the calming mood of contentment is hard to come by. We wonder: when is enough *enough?* Something always remains to be done. Here developing explicit strategies of physical relaxation—stretching, simple movements of yoga or tai chi, even a walk around the block—may be required if we are to benefit from the calming system of physiological regulation.

In other situations, too, intentional practices of self-calming may be called on to regulate our threat-protection emotions. Initially we feel a surge of anger at a suspected insult, but then we realize no insult was intended. Now, left with the residual arousals of the anger, how are we to calm ourselves? Delayed in traffic or kept waiting in the busy physician's office—these everyday frustrations, too, generate an emotional response. As anxiety builds, muscles in the shoulders and stomach tighten. In instances like this, a simple discipline of slow, deep breathing often comes to our rescue. This practice evokes the calming system that counteracts our physiological response to threat. Anger and anxiety are essential capacities in our emotional repertoire, but developing our own strategies of calming helps keep these healthy resources in check.

Our management of these emotional domains is not a private affair. As Christians, we enjoy a rich heritage that seeks to form our hearts in these powerful emotions. Biblical stories, religious education and liturgical celebrations all reinforce a particular vision of these emotions. So the Hebrew bible speaks repeatedly of the Jews' desire for

God, just as the psalms repeatedly express the fear and anxiety that haunt eras of slavery and exile. The Christian Gospels again and again exhort believers, "do not be afraid," seeking to calm anxious hearts. And as we saw in the figure above, Jesus endorses the same calming effect: "Peace I leave with you, my peace I give you." Our liturgical life, at its best, endorses these motivating moods: creating communal celebrations of hope and longing; acknowledging the social forces that threaten a life of faith; and seeking the peace and calm that accompanies our trust in God.

Emotions and the Life of the Spirit

To love morally, courageously, generously, while facing the unavoidable fragility of our human lives, we need a continuing program of spiritual askesis [discipline], which will replace fear with trust, which will address our vulnerability by transforming it into a receptivity and openness.
—JOHN COTTINGHAM

There is general agreement today that no emotions are dedicated solely to religious faith or practice. No emotions are unique to any one religious heritage. These arousals are common property of our species. Yet emotions are, in fact, often linked with religious sensitivity. Our everyday emotions sometimes carry intuitions of *something more* in life. Diana Fritz Cates describes this phenomenon: A religious emotion arises when our "interest and attention are drawn beyond" an ordinary feeling "toward the hidden source of its power, toward the ultimate cause or reason for its being, or toward a horizon of meaning (only partly visible) against which the object takes on a significance that it would not otherwise have."

Moved by gratitude, for example, this feeling may expand in a sense of thankfulness that extends beyond this concrete relationship. Or angry at a particular injustice, we feel this emotion widen into resentment toward God for allowing such evil to occur. Or affection shared with our beloved expands our heart as our love broadens in wider compassion for all those who suffer. In these examples the movements toward transcendence do not replace the basic emotion at their core. Instead, the everyday arousal seems to possess the potential to open us to a more expansive experience.

The emotions of wonder and awe open the self-absorbed heart to the *something else* and *something more* that bear the weighty title of *transcendence*. Without such an emotion it would be difficult to exit the confines of the obvious and the ordinary. Wonder and awe, in turn, engender the religious practice of reverence, though here, too, reverence is not restricted to the religious domain. The artist, the scientist, the explorer often respond in reverence to the wonder of the world.

The emotion of compassion lifts us out of self-concern and focuses our attention on the vulnerable "other." Here begins all morality, civic and religious. The emotion of hope, initially focused on a particular improvement, may expand into visions and promises of other possibilities. It was hope that triggered in the prophet Isaiah's imagination the ideal of "swords beaten into plowshares." These and other emotions serve as portals to religious experience, as well as to the resilient resources we know as virtues.

In his influential book *A Secular Age*, Charles Taylor describes the challenges and opportunities that may lie in our common future. Many Christians today are "looking for a more direct experience of the sacred, for greater immediacy, spontaneity, and spiritual depths." They are "seeking a kind of unity and wholeness of the self, a reclaiming of the place of feeling, against the one-sided pre-eminence of reason, and a reclaiming of the body and its pleasures from the inferior and often guilt-ridden place it had been allowed in the disciplined, instrumental identity."

Near the end of this important discussion, Taylor states again his vision of humanity's shared hope: "One could say we look for new and unprecedented itineraries. Understanding our time in Christian terms is partly to discern these new paths, opened by pioneers who have discovered a way through the particular labyrinthine landscape we live in, its thickets and trackless wastes, to God." In the chapters ahead we trace the ways that emotions of wonder, appreciation, hope and mercy may light this landscape and direct our movements on the spiritual journey.

2

Wonder, Awe and Reverence

*I will call to mind the deeds of the Lord. I will
remember your wonders of old. I will meditate
on all your work and muse on your mighty
deeds. You are the God who works wonders.*

—Psalm 77

Wonder and awe are positive emotions that arrest our attention,
open our eyes to a dazzling creation and serve as doors to the sacred.
These emotional arousals alert us to boundaries in life where our
knowledge comes to a halt and our curiosity intensifies. We may
experience both meanings of wonder as we stand at the edge of the
Grand Canyon. At first we are simply astonished; we are stopped in
our tracks and filled with awe. Then we may be moved to wonder—
how has this come about? Now our awe has become inquisitive,
wonder as curious. We are strangely attracted by what exceeds our
comprehension.

Historian Caroline Bynum names this experience: "We wonder at
what we cannot in any sense incorporate, consume or encompass in
our mental categories." Wonder stirs us out of complacency and ushers
us beyond our comfort zone; we are at once thrilled and disoriented.
Wonder and awe often arise together, eliciting practices of respect
and reverence.

Humans are designed with this capacity to be amazed. Robert
Fuller notes: "Wonder . . . is one of the brain's hardwired programs
that respond to unexpected phenomena." The gift of wonder and
amazement is "heightened interest, [that] momentarily suspends
habitual ways of looking at the world and instead lures people into
new and creative engagement with their surroundings." When we are
amazed we pay closer attention, and this attention may well give way

to a new appreciation of the world around us. "Experiences of wonder enable us to view the world independent of its relationships to our own immediate needs. They thereby foster empathy and compassion."

Philosopher Martha Nussbaum traces the early origins of this emotion in Western culture. In the ancient Greek dramatists wonder is "that which inspires awe . . . it can be used of the dazzling brilliance of the human intellect, of the monstrousness of evil, of the terrible power of fate." Sophocles has his heroine Antigone describe the play of this emotion in humanity:

> Many are the wonders, none is more wonderful than what is man . . . a clever fellow is man . . . he has a way against every-thing . . . Only against death can he call on no means of escape.

Nussbaum describes this drama as "a play about teaching and learning, about changing one's vision of the world, about losing one's grip on what looked like secure truth and learning a more elusive kind of wisdom." It is this losing one's grip and simultane-ously gaining a more elusive kind of wisdom that lies at the core of wonder.

The rich nuances of wonder that were celebrated in pre-modern cultures lost favor as early scientists increasingly enshrined scientific analysis as the single avenue to a trustworthy understanding of the world.

> By the late 16th century, European scientists began to look down on wonder; they began to see it as the mark of a childish mind, whereas the mature scientist went about coolly catalog-ing the laws of the world. Scientists may tell us in their memoirs about their private sense of wonder, but the everyday world of the scientist is one that rigidly separates facts from values and emotions.

The Return of Wonder

By the second half of the twentieth century, science began to lose its single-minded obsession with instrumental reason. A richer apprecia-tion of the strength and limits of the scientific method—exemplified in the work of Thomas Kuhn and Stephen Toulmin—opened space for the return of wonder to late modern consciousness. A more sophis-ticated scientific appreciation of the natural world provoked wonder at our planet's profound fragility, its extravagant immensity and its mysterious interconnections.

Environmentalist Rachel Carson returned wonder to center stage. In her 1962 classic *Silent Spring* Carson exposed the devastation that poisonous pesticides and other pollutants had brought to natural water supplies, resulting in the death of both wildlife and plant species. In her examination of the fragility of nature she argued that "most of us walk unseeing through the world, unaware alike of its beauties, its wonders, and the strange and sometimes terrible intensity of the lives that are being lived about us." Her compelling descriptions shocked readers into a new consciousness of the earth's fragility. Carson's reflections on the vital complexity of natural soil, with its intricate balance of chemicals and living organisms that renders the fields fertile, replaced "common sense" and superficial images of groundcover as inert *dirt*. Suddenly the earth was re-imagined, no longer a self-sufficient machine but a vulnerable organism.

These experiences of wonder led Carson to develop an ethic of aesthetic appreciation and responsiveness. This ethical emotion, she insists, awakens a passion for "some universal truth that lies just beyond our grasp . . . (a meaning that) haunts and ever eludes us, and in its very pursuit we approach the ultimate mystery of Life itself."

In recent decades astronomers and cosmologists have described a universe whose immensity is extravagant and awe inspiring. How are we to comprehend a cosmos that embraces millions of galaxies and billions of stars? What does such immensity and extravagance mean? Why is there so much? And, perhaps the deepest wonder, why is there anything at all? Philosopher Charles Taylor adds his voice to this chorus of amazement at the world we inhabit: "The wonder is not only at the stupendous whole, but at the way in which we emerge, in one way fragile and insignificant, and yet capable of grasping the whole . . . One can even say that a kind of piety arises here, in which we recognize that for all our detachment in objectivizing thought, we ultimately belong to this whole, and return to it."

Portals to Wonder

Awe and wonder, our emotional responses to extraordinary experience, are what psychologists now discuss as evolved capacities. These moral resources, expressed today in heightened responsibility for our extravagant but fragile planet, have developed over many millions of years. The capacity for wonder is expressed today in many ways, perhaps especially through our fascination with beauty, music and numbers.

Beauty is both a pleasure for its own sake and a threshold to wonder. Astonished at the beauty that surrounds us we ask: What is beauty for? Elaine Scarry comments, "Beauty welcomes us; makes us attentive." She continues, "It is as though beautiful things have been placed here and there throughout the world to serve as small wake-up calls to perception."

Beautiful things bring us to a halt. "At the moment we see something beautiful, we undergo a radical decentering." Our attention is drawn elsewhere and "all the space formerly in the service of protecting, guarding, advancing the self (or its "prestige") is now free to be in the service of something else."

Music likewise serves as a portal to wonder. Stirring rhythms suggest realms of mysterious order and registers of feelings for which we have no words. George Steiner comments that music "is brimful of meanings which will not translate into logical structures or verbal expression." Music speaks to "intimations of a source and destination somehow outside the range of man."

Part of the thrall of music is the intricate arrangement of ratios that bind chords and notes. H. E. Huntley describes the intuitions spawned by our wonder at the orderly world of numbers. As we appreciate the play of numbers in music, mathematics, architecture and astronomy, "the conviction grows stronger that we have chanced on an unexplored world which, like the universe around us, appears to have no boundaries. There must, we speculate, be other discoveries to be made here by the inquiring mind."

Music, dance and other symbolic gestures come together in ceremony to arrest our attention and invite our appreciation of what we cannot fully comprehend. Humans long ago discovered the ability to orchestrate movement, sound and symbols to evoke feelings of reverence. Rituals of grief, of thanks, of supplication rise up to help us savor the wonderful and the awesome. The goal might be a patriotism; a parade of vast numbers of soldiers followed by a frightening array of armament and accompanied by flags and rousing music is meant to arouse wonder and respect. And the Easter celebration with its ritual movement from the darkness of night into light, its recollection of creation and its other symbols of new life evokes for the faithful renewed wonder and gratitude.

The Religious Emotion of Awe

Clap your hands, all you peoples; shout to God with loud songs of joy, for the Lord, the Most High, is awesome.

—PSALM 47

At the heart of religious life resides a complex emotion that is both deeply unsettling and strangely uplifting. This emotion—of awe, astonishment, wonder—is aroused when we stumble onto the Mystery that envelopes and transcends us. Jonathan Haidt and Dacher Keltner suggest an intriguing definition of this emotion: "In the upper reaches of pleasure and on the boundary of fear is a little studied emotion—awe. Awe is felt about diverse events and objects, from waterfalls to childbirth to scenes of devastation." The force of this experience may so disorient us that we call it terrifying, but it entails much more than fear.

The story of Job offers a dramatic version of this experience. Literary critic Robert Alter observes that this brief text contains no mention of Israel, but it was "a book of such power that Hebrew readers soon came to feel they couldn't do without it, however vehement its swerve from the views of the biblical majority."

Sure of his own uprightness, Job demands of God an explanation for his suffering. Finally, God tires of such presumption and staggers Job with an onslaught of questions: Where were you when the world was created? Have you ever caused the dawn? Ever visited the storehouse of the snows? (Jb 38–41). Job is confounded. Humbled, he confesses: I have misspoken; I am out of my depths. "I have uttered what I did not understand, things too wonderful for me which I did not know . . . I regret my actions and repent in dust and ashes" (Jb 42:3, 6). Job's experience is a mixed emotion, blending fright, amazement and awe. It is not a fear that warns of an immediate danger, nor is it worry about a threatening future. Instead, it is the bewilderment that registers as we face certain uncanny experiences, when we recognize that we are in over our heads.

The emotion of awe appears throughout the New Testament in the stories that attempt to account for the extraordinary attraction and power of Jesus. Jesus' actions at times startled the disciples, at times disoriented them. As it dawned on them that Jesus was much more than a devout healer, the question arose about how to communicate this realization. In the gospel account of the transfiguration we see their effort to present this experience in symbolic form. Ascending a mountain together, his three companions suddenly are presented with a striking scenario. The gospel story is ornamented with the pyrotechnics of a mythic tale: they find themselves on a mountain (a place whose elevation allows further vision or revelation); Jesus' clothes turn dazzling white (signaling special illumination). Suddenly Jesus' appearance is radiant, and he seems to be talking with ancient prophets. The disciples, staggered by this display, show signs of an intense befuddlement. Symptoms multiply as they enter a kind of stupor—the Greek word here is *hypnos*, as in hypnosis. Peter suggests they set up tents, but his disorientation is signaled with the added remark, "not knowing what he was saying" (Lk 9:33). In the account in Matthew's Gospel we see more signs of confusion: "They fell on their faces and were filled with awe" (Mt 17:6). Then Jesus tells his friends not to be afraid, and suddenly the Jesus they see is the one with whom they are familiar. He is again their everyday companion, but now they know he is also much more, something they do not pretend to comprehend.

A similar range of emotions floods the women who visit the tomb of Jesus after his death and burial. Finding the tomb empty they are astonished and frightened. What could this mean? Has someone stolen his body, or is something yet more amazing taking place? In Luke's account we read that they are "perplexed." Their hearts are jolted and, Mark's Gospel reports, "they fled from the tomb, for terror and amazement had seized them; and they said nothing to anyone for they were much afraid" (Mk 16:8). The Greek words in the New Testament suggest trembling and ecstasy. The women were beside themselves with a frightening and euphoric disorientation.

As religious institutions hand on the faith, they often domesticate the unsettling elements in such stories, smoothing out emotional extremes. Over time a religious people may focus its faith on observing established rules; its ceremonies and rituals are gradually emptied of extravagant gestures, and its spiritual life settles into a placid, if boring, routine. Awe and wonder are casualties of this routinization of belief.

The Psychology of Awe

Psychologists Haidt and Keltner offer a definition of this compelling emotion: "Awe involves being in the presence of something powerful, along with associated feelings of submission. Awe also involves a difficulty of comprehension, along with associated feelings of confusion, surprise, and wonder." In their analysis two themes are at play: "The stimulus is vast and . . . requires accommodation." By vastness they mean something "much larger than the self"—whether this is a frightening storm, a sober diagnosis of a mortal disease or, as in our reflection here, the startling awareness of God's powerful presence. By "accommodation" they mean the need for "adjusting mental structures that cannot assimilate a new experience." The biblical accounts of the disciples at the transfiguration and the empty tomb certainly portray a profound accommodation. Haidt and Keltner conclude, "Awe can transform people and reorient their lives, goals, and values." Without doubt the astonishment undergone by the disciples of Jesus, then and now, does reorient lives.

For their own example of this emotion Haidt and Keltner turn to an ancient Indian religious classic. In the Bhagavad Gita the hero, Arjuna, is about to lead his soldiers into battle. At this point he loses his nerve and refuses to go forward. The god Krishna reminds him of his duty and explains the movements of the universe in order to encourage Arjuna. Arjuna then asks Krishna to allow him to see the inner workings of the universe. So Krishna gives him a vision of the universe as it really is.

This vision elicits in Arjuna something like a psychotic break or psychedelic experience. He sees gods, suns and infinite time and space. He is filled with amazement. His hair stands on end. Disoriented, he struggles to describe the wonders he is beholding. Arjuna is clearly in a state of awe when he says, "Things never seen before have I seen, and ecstatic is my joy; yet fear and trembling perturb my mind."

Haidt and Keltner suggest five distinct nuances that flavor the experience of this emotion. Awe may well be "flavored by feelings of fear" in the experience of an electrical storm. This differs significantly from the calmer appreciation of an awesome sunset. Second, awe is "flavored with aesthetic pleasure" when we encounter beauty. Delight and joy attend this kind of awe, with fear nowhere in sight. Third, we undergo awe when we observe some extraordinary skill that inspires both admiration and amazement. An exceptional athlete might trigger this arousal of awe. Fourth, awe blends with elevation when we observe an action of moral virtue—an act of compassion or forgiveness. Haidt and Keltner suggest: "Elevation appears to be a member of the family of awe-related states."

And fifth, these psychologists acknowledge the awe released by what they call "supernatural causality." This, they suggest, is the awe that will "flavor an experience with an element of the uncanny." Here they come full circle, to the place where awe mingles with fear. "The uncanny is usually terrifying."

In these extraordinary moments awe brings us up against a barrier or boundary to our own existence. Pressing against it—as Job did, or as we do when looking into a storm or approaching death—we are gripped by a range of emotions. These feelings, whatever their names, mark the place where we reach a limit and something greater and more mysterious begins. The sharp sense of this edge both excites and frightens us. We fall silent, not wishing to speak; we savor something that is beyond our grasp but within our vision. Missing these brief glimpses, our lives would be less rich and we would be less human.

Profound feelings of elevation and humility often accompany these emotional experiences. In moments of awe we feel buoyed up, even exhilarated. Simultaneously we are brought low, not in humiliation, but with a profound sense of our true significance in the face of a fathomless universe. Philip Wheelwright says it this way: "Awe is ambivalent emotion, compounded of wonder and humility; the wonder keeps the emotion alive and the mind open, while humility restrains the wonder from slipping into idle curiosity."

The Practice of Reverence

Reverence is an ancient virtue that survives among us in half forgotten patterns of civility, in moments of inarticulate awe, and in nostalgia for the lost ways of traditional cultures.
—PAUL WOODRUFF

Reverence is often associated with religion: the deep bows of monks or the solemn gestures of the minister at a funeral. But this emotion is part of every human's repertoire. Paul Woodruff writes: "It is a natural mistake to think that reverence belongs to religion. It belongs, instead, to community. Wherever people try to act together, they hedge themselves around with some form of ceremony or good manners, and the observance of this can be an act of reverence." Acts of reverence follow naturally on experiences that are awesome and wonderful.

Reverence has fallen out of favor in contemporary Western culture. In this environment, steeped in ideals of autonomy and resistant to all forms of constraint, irreverence is prized as a sign of spontaneity and freedom from the pieties of the past. Irreverence has become, along with a sense of entitlement, a hallmark of contemporary culture. Irreverence disrespects, on principle, inherited values, social classes and their privileged players (princes, priests, judges) who have been too long uncritically esteemed. For many today, outmoded titles of social pieties—Reverend, Your Honor, Your Excellency—seem to cry out for irreverent response. Humor trades in irreverence, pulling down the privileged few who pretend to stand superior to the rest of us. Comedians deploy banter and mockery as exercises in irreverence meant to entertain. In the media today irony and smugness leave little room for reverence of any kind.

Ian Barbour laments a scientific mentality that has fostered this irreverence: "The experience of reverence and wonder is not nurtured by the technological mentality that looks on the world—and even on human beings—as objects to be controlled and manipulated. As man's ancient dependence on nature has been replaced by various forms of dominion and mastery, the destructive consequences of this arrogance have become increasingly evident in the despoliation of the environment." But he retains hope that "a new recognition of interdependence and a new respect for nature may be ecologically beneficial and at the same time foster the sort of humility which is a pre-requisite for religious reverence." In acts of reverence we choose to hold the whole of creation in a more generous embrace.

A capacity for reverence depends on some comfort with our limitations. Paul Woodruff writes: "Reverence begins in a deep understanding of human limitations; from this grows the capacity to be in awe of whatever you believe lies outside our control—God, truth, justice, nature, even death. The capacity for awe, as it grows, brings with it the capacity for respecting fellow human beings."

A recent development at Northwestern University Medical School serves as a secular example of reverence. Medical students conclude their participation in an anatomy course with a ceremony that celebrates the life of the deceased person whose body they have dissected. Music, poems and memorial prayers are offered in tribute to the person whose last exercise of generosity was to provide this body for medical study. At the end of the ceremony students are given a white rose that they, in turn, place in a vase as they thank the individual deceased donor. In this exercise of respect a clinical exercise and medical examination of tissue and bones are raised to a fully human act, attuned to the generosity of the donor.

Wonder and awe are positive emotions with religious resonance. Undergoing these emotions we search for symbolic means to express our respect and even reverence. This complex of wonder, awe and reverence abides close to the heart of every spiritual tradition and every spiritual life.

3

The Rehabilitation of Emotion

It is my belief that the psychological sciences are on the verge of a spiritual revolution . . . Research that documents the role of spirituality in personal and social well-being will play a major role in this revolution.

—ROBERT EMMONS

A dramatic shift in attitudes toward emotion is evident in both Christian reflection and in academic research. Today, disciplines ranging from philosophy to the neurosciences have taken up study of emotions, recognizing their crucial role in moral and spiritual life. Antonio Demasio recalls the background of this shift, "Not long ago people thought of emotions as old stuff, as just feelings—feeling that had little to do with rational decision making, or that got in the way of it." Martha Nussbaum has designated this development "the rehabilitation of emotion in practical reasoning." Emotions, we are coming to see, attune humans to their environment. "They embody ways of interpreting the world."

Robert Solomon was among the first to document the important cognitive contribution of the emotions and passions. In *The Passions* he argued that the emotions "are not irrational . . . but they are themselves judgments of the most important kind." He continues, "These emotions, and the passions in general, are the very core of our existence, the system of meanings and values within which our lives either develop and grow or starve and stagnate."

Nussbaum emphasizes the rational character of the emotions. "Passions such as fear, anger, grief and love are not blind surges of affect . . . They are, in fact, intelligent and discriminating elements of the personality." She adds, "In the process of wise judgment rich emotional response is a mark not of irrationality but of rich or complete rationality." Elsewhere she presses home the point: "Emotions are not just the fuel that powers the psychological mechanism of a reasoning creature, they are parts, highly complex and messy parts, of this creature's reasoning itself."

Daniel Siegel summarizes an emerging consensus among psychologists of emotions' essential role in every form of reflection: "all information processing is emotional, in that emotion is the energy that drives, organizes, amplifies, and attenuates cognitive activity and in turn is the experience and expression of this activity." Siegel concludes, "The common distinction made between thought and feeling, cognition and emotion, is artificial and potentially harmful to our understanding of mental processes."

Emotions and Moral Life

For many centuries linking the words *emotions* and *moral* seemed to involve a contradiction. Emotion was precisely what was *not moral* about humans; eruptions of anger or fear or pride—or, even more, sexual arousal—were objects of moral sanction. In their best guise, emotions were thought to be amoral; in their worst appearances, they were immoral.

The conventional definition of the human person as a *rational animal* drove a wedge between reason—the glory of humanity, its light and its promise—and our *animal nature,* home to disruptive passions and unruly emotions. Paul described his own inner conflict, a struggle that seemed to validate the spiritual rupture at our core: "I do not do what I want, but I do the very things I hate . . . I see in my members another law at war with the law of my mind" (Rom 7:15, 23). To be sure, the havoc wreaked by overwhelming emotion is familiar to us all: fear mushrooming into debilitating dread; pride leading to a chronic self-absorption. What positive contribution could such emotions make to the moral life? Living virtuously seemed to demand the mastery, perhaps even the suppression, of passion and emotion. Here Christian belief mirrored the Stoic conviction that endorsed an ideal of rational tranquility.

In the last decades of the twentieth century this negative view of the moral impact of the emotions began to change. William Spohn urged Christian scholars to look again at the positive role of emotions. "It is regrettable that moral theology has neglected the role that emotions play in the moral life." But, he noted, "in recent years, ethics has become less suspicious of emotion's role in moral experience." Spohn argued that "reason and emotion tutor one another," even if many experiences of emotions "are primarily intuitive." He notes that religious traditions have two powerful resources to assist their task of "schooling the affections." These are the biblical accounts of powerful emotions that have supported the life of the spirit, and religious rituals that practically engage believers in communal expressions of gratitude and grief.

Identifying the Moral Emotions

Psychologist Jonathan Haidt observes, "Any emotion that leads people to care about the world, and to support, enforce, or improve its integrity should be considered a moral emotion, even when the actions taken are not nice." He offers examples: "Moral intuitions in the form of embodied emotions like compassion, gratitude, embarrassment, and awe . . . serve as powerful moral guides." These upheavals, Haidt continues, "propel us to protect the foundations of moral communities—concerns over fairness, obligations, virtue, kindness, and reciprocity." In fact, we may say that the designation *moral* applies to all *"those emotions that are linked to the interests or welfare either of society as a whole or at least of persons other than the judge or agent."*

We sometimes experience these moral intuitions as moral needs, as Susan Neiman notes. "We have moral needs, needs so strong they can override our instincts for self-preservation . . . They include the need to express reverence and the need to express outrage . . . the need to see our own lives as stories with meaning—meaning we impose on the world, a crucial source of human dignity—without which we hold our lives to be worthless."

This discussion of moral emotions marks a return to a more holistic vision of human knowing, to include emotional sensitivity, intuitive insight and rational reflection. Moral emotions involve more than physiological arousal. These emotions fuse cognitive value judgments with strong feelings, motivating us to engage life in constructive and healing ways.

Not every emotional arousal has moral overtones, but the stirring of compassion and gratitude and shame very frequently inform our moral lives. The emotional stirring of empathy for a suffering person moves us to act with compassion. The arousal is not only interior and emotional; it prompts moral actions of care and compassion. Neiman makes explicit the link between emotion and morality: "The emotional responses to others' suffering that we share with apes are building blocks of the complex structures of human morality." Our primate relatives share some of these basic capacities. "The sense of justice, the feeling of sympathy, the urge to share, the capacity for gratitude all start right here."

The Moral Emotion of Anger

Haidt argues that "anger is usually thought of as an *immoral* emotion . . . But for every spectacular display of angry violence there are many more mundane cases of people indignantly standing up for what is right, or angrily demanding justice for themselves or others."

Anger makes a moral claim: a wrong has been done that must be set right. And as Haidt reminds us, "Anger is not just a response to insults, in which case it would be just a guardian of self-esteem." More broadly, anger arouses us to remedy an intolerable situation. Anger flares in the face of injustice—unfair treatment of ourselves or other people, actions that attack our sense of decency or fair play, situations that show contempt for values at the core of our own world view. Moral indignation alerts us to injustice; the anger it sparks fuels our courageous response. Befriended and tamed, anger becomes a powerful ally.

The Moral Emotion of Pride

Pride points to the pleasure we take in the achievements of our children and colleagues as well as delight in our own successes. This positive emotion adds our voice in the chorus of praise for the goodness of creation. Yet this emotion, too, found its way onto the list of the seven deadly sins.

Augustine was a chief promoter of pride as sinful; for him, pride was a manifestation of the creature's rejection of the obedience owed to the Creator. Centuries later Thomas Aquinas reinstated pride as a moral emotion, even a Christian virtue. Describing the virtue of magnanimity (greatness of heart), Aquinas wrote of the "great things" to which God invites humanity. And while refusing to embrace our Spirit-inspired ambition, or turning away from the risks of such endeavors, might be registered by some as humility, this should not be seen as Christian virtue. The moral emotion of pride celebrates our status as created in the image of God and supports our greatness of heart.

The Moral Emotion of Elevation

Seeing someone else act with compassion or courage, we are often moved. We may feel a warming in the chest and tightening in the throat. Some of us experience tears welling up. The moral emotion here has been named *elevation*. Jonathan Haidt's research into this positive emotion found people reporting "physical feelings in their chests, especially warm, pleasant, or tingling feelings, and they were more likely to report wanting to help others, and to become better people themselves." In elevation we feel uplifted, encouraged, stirred with admiration and a desire to "go and do likewise."

Elevation is considered a moral emotion because it responds to human excellence, especially those altruistic actions that support human interconnectedness. Responding to what is good in human nature—acts of selflessness, courage, moral integrity—elevation refutes our world-weary cynicism. Elevation can reinforce, even reorient, our own value commitments. When we experience this emotion, many of us feel personally motivated to become better, not just to mimic the particular action we have witnessed, but to respond generously to others in the future.

Elevation is also recognized as one of the healing emotions. Haidt observes: "Powerful moments of elevation sometimes seem to push a mental 'reset button' wiping out feelings of cynicism and replacing them with feelings of hope, love, and optimism, and a sense of moral inspiration." In elevation we are drawn out of ourselves, not in care for the afflicted, as in compassion, but in admiration for excellence and a desire to act in ways that affirm our own better nature.

Elevation heals by broadening our sense of relatedness. We feel more connected to humanity. A deeper appreciation of our shared vulnerability is coupled with renewed confidence in the human spirit. Elevation heals by reminding us of what is good in other people and in our world. Elevation often moves us toward other people, opening us to new relationships. We are drawn not only to those whose exemplary behavior has stirred our heart, but more broadly to others who share our common humanity. And elevation can sometimes move us to tears when our hearts are touched by the goodness around us.

Moral Emotions as Evolved Capacities

The rehabilitation of emotion has led to a new interest in emotions as evolved capacities—innate resources in the human species that have been honed over millions of years. The interest in evolved capacities brings a more sophisticated appreciation of evolution's dynamic. More than competition and survival of the fittest are at play. Neiman argues that our evolutionary endowment includes not only proclivities for violence and selfishness but tendencies for trust and hope. "We are born with capacities that are continuous with those of other animals. Apes show the capacity for generosity and altruism. It is wrong to link our negative traits (savagery) with other animals, but not our positive traits (generosity)." She adds: "The emotional responses to others' suffering that we share with apes are building blocks of the complex structure of human morality."

The record shows that human evolution includes developing strategies of cooperation. David Brooks comments: "Humans don't just care about themselves. We also care about loyalty, respect, traditions, religions. We are all the descendants of successful cooperators." Brooks concludes, "As Darwin himself speculated, competition among groups has turned us into cooperative, empathetic and altruistic creatures."

George Vaillant describes this evolution of moral capacities: "It all began more than 200 million years ago when faithless, walnut-brained, untrusting, humorless, cold-blooded reptiles slowly evolved into warm-blooded, child-nurturing, faithful, hopeful, large-brained mammals capable of play, joy, attachment, and trust in their parents to care for them rather than do them for lunch."

By evolved capacities we refer to in-built potentials for certain kinds of behaviors. Language is, perhaps, the best example of such a capacity. This potential is hardwired into our brains but awaits social contact to be activated. Humans lack the instincts that instruct the spider in the building of its web. The spider needs no training in this skill. Humans' capacities tend to be more flexible and more dependent on social shaping. As Keltner observes, "Our capacity for virtue and concern over right and wrong are wired into our bodies." These "emotions provide rapid intuitions about fairness, harm, virtue, kindness and purity." He concludes, "Emotions are guides to moral reasoning, to ethical action in the fast, face-to-face exchanges of our social life. Reason and passion are collaborators in the meaningful life."

The Evolved Capacity of Hope

Hope is a curious capacity that redirects our concern from the present, with its many worries and desires, to the future—even to a future that lies beyond the horizon of our own life. If the evolved capacity of compassion lifts our attention from ourselves to care for others, hope focuses our energy on what yet might be.

Vaillant describes hope's distinctive perspective: "Hope reflects the capacity for one's loving, lyrical, limbic memory of the past to become attached to *the memory of the future*. This capacity occurs within our most recently evolved frontal lobes." He concludes: "Our capacity to anticipate, to mourn in advance, to plant seeds, and to plan for the future are all capacities based in our frontal lobes. Only an integrated brain can hope that agriculture can really work, that seeds planted in bleak spring will bear fruit next autumn."

The Evolved Capacity of Laughter

In humans, laughter is a multipurpose behavior, ranging from the child's delightful squeal to the cynic's derision. Physically, laughter relieves tension in the body and promotes relaxation. Aristotle included *wittiness* among the moral virtues. This virtuous capacity for wit—a ready and tactful ability to evoke laughter among friends—occupies the middle ground between the extremes of boorish humor and humorlessness. Laughter itself is contagious; we laugh most often when we are with other people. And laughter spreads rapidly through a group. This social arousal serves many purposes. Keltner observes, "Laughter builds cooperative bonds vital to group living." In addition, "laughter signals appreciation and shared understanding."

In his classic analysis Aristotle judged that laughter serves the larger purposes of play and rest, both essential to a flourishing life. But laughter was disapproved and discouraged by many early church writers. Again, this was graphically the case for Augustine, who remembered laughter as mainly a tool for derision or ridicule.

But as effective comedians know, laughter also heals. Garrison Keillor, for example, skillfully shapes his humor to transform caustic complaint. He writes often of his strict religious upbringing, which has left him with an inability to rejoice and enjoy life. "I am constantly adjusting my feelings downward to achieve that fine balance of caution and melancholy." And in this exaggerated complaint audiences hear echoes of their own regrets. But for many, gentle laughter softens lingering resentment and begins to heal old wounds.

Drama critic John Lahr describes this healing force of laughter in "The Laughing Cure," published in the *New Yorker*: "When we say laughter lifts our spirits, we mean it works as a sort of stage-managed resurrection—we are somehow taken out of ourselves . . . and in that instant, life becomes luminous again."

The Evolved Capacity of Catharsis—"Healing without Cure"

Of the capacities that have evolved in the long history of humanity, perhaps the most curious is our appreciation of vulnerability. Vulnerability is a constant companion on the human journey. Our appreciation is on display in the drama or film that artfully depicts deep sorrow or tragedy. The classic Greek tragedies *Antigone* and *Oedipus* serve as examples, as does the 1993 film *Schindler's List*. Leaving the theater after these masterful productions we are sobered, even saddened. Yet many of us are also consoled and enriched. What has happened here?

Aristotle identified this complex of emotions as *catharsis*, a Greek word meaning "purification" or "purging." From such a drama, he indicated, "all must get a sort of catharsis and be enlightened together with pleasure." Martha Nussbaum describes this aspect of great art as the effort to take the measure of human grief. These enactments do not dissolve the perennial distress that plagues humanity, but somehow that malaise is humanized, made more bearable. She describes the effect of artful performance as "healing without cure."

Popular entertainment in contemporary American culture shows little interest in catharsis. Horror movies evoke the shock of artificial terror; rock concerts trigger a reliable rush of emotions; soap operas service our sentimental tendencies. These performances offer distraction from immediate concerns and momentary relief from boredom without approaching the healing power of catharsis. Yet even in our day genuine artists in many media are able to evoke this experience. At the core of this emotional stirring is a paradoxical pleasure, as we savor—ruefully—the mystery of our mortal lives.

Spirituality and the Human Sciences: A Developing Friendship

For much of the twentieth century the human sciences and religious faith had little in common. Suspicion reigned on both sides. Many psychologists were disposed to interpret religious experience as superstition and emotionalism. Evolutionary biologists often explained religion as a relic of an earlier era, likely to disappear as humankind reached maturity. Religious believers, defensive in the face of such condescension, tended to distance themselves from the pronouncements of scientific research.

In recent decades these rigid attitudes have softened. Many in the psychological sciences now recognize religious aspiration as an essential dynamic in the human search for meaning and purpose. Upon closer examination, spiritual devotion has been acknowledged as a positive element in human flourishing. A new interest in *moral psychology* shows a surprising openness to *moral theology*, as both disciplines explore the role of virtues and character strengths in shaping human life.

Two social scientists exemplify this new détente. Robert Emmons is a leader in the fields of personality psychology and the psychology of religion. From his earlier focus on happiness, he has come to a more systematic study of the contributions of spirituality and religion to psychological health. Emmons recognizes that "spirituality . . . is thought to encompass a search for meaning, for unity, for connectedness, for transcendence . . . Embedding one's finite life within a grander, all-encompassing narrative appears to be a universal human need, as the inability to do so leads to despair and self-destructive behavior." He argues for "a robust connection between personal well-being and a concern for the spiritual. The *faith factor* emerges as a significant contributor to quality-of-life indicators such as life satisfaction, happiness, self-esteem, hope and optimism, and meaning in life."

In recent years George Vaillant, a life-long student of human development, has turned to the study of spirituality and its role in human maturing. His work in this area focuses on "an individual's sense of connection with a transcendent power (be it a single deity or anything else considered to be *larger* than one's self) with feelings of awe, gratitude, compassion and forgiveness." Vaillant's interest in the evolution of moral emotions forms a bridge to his understanding links between emotion and religious maturing. "Mammalian evolution has hardwired the human brain for subjective spiritual/religious emotional experience." This is especially the case with the positive emotions. "The human capacity for positive emotions is what makes us spiritual." Among these spiritually significant emotions he includes "awe, love, joy, hope, faith/trust, forgiveness, gratitude and compassion."

Researchers in the human sciences today are investigating the role of social institutions in the formation of moral character and personal well-being. Many of these scholars give focused attention to religious institutions as *schools of the emotions*. In these settings community members are instructed in the virtues of patience and courage; they are invited into practices of compassion and forgiveness. Psychologists and other educators have come to fuller appreciation of this formative effect, which serves to broaden and build the emotions essential for human flourishing.

4

Anger, Courage and Hope

Courage is a complex resolve to go forward in the face of adversity. Courage invites us to tame our fear, temper our anger and embrace our hope that justice and compassion may find a secure place in the world.

We think of courage as a heroic virtue, the strength at play in truly extraordinary lives—Socrates, Gandhi, Mother Teresa, Martin Luther King Jr. But even apart from these exceptional models we find evidence of humble bravery in ourselves—occasions when we have been willing to confront a daunting challenge. Anyone committed to significant values can anticipate a call to courageous action.

Annie Dillard observes: "There were no formerly heroic times, and there was no formerly pure generation. There is no one here but us chickens, and so it has always been." She reminds us of the contradictions in our humanity; we are "a people busy and powerful, knowledgeable, ambivalent, important, fearful, and self-aware . . . who pray for their loved ones, and long to flee misery and skip death." And while this non-heroic account of human life is accurate, we can still take comfort in the recognition that even ordinary folk—like us—possess the capacity for courage. By tempering our anger, restraining our fear, and reinforcing our hopes, courage helps us pursue our deepest values.

Courage in the Life of Jesus

We begin our exploration of courage with the memory of Jesus facing the consequences of his own vocation. As it became clear that his ministry of teaching and healing was drawing the antagonism of powerful members in his society, Jesus struggled to stay on course, to do what he felt called to do. "From that time on, Jesus began to show his disciples that he must go to Jerusalem and undergo great suffering" (Mt 16:21). But as he announces his recommitment to this dangerous path, his friend and colleague Peter objects, telling him not to go to Jerusalem, that now is not a good time. Jesus suddenly explodes in anger: "Get behind me, Satan! You are a stumbling block to me" (Mt 16:23). Harsh language for a close friend, denouncing him as the devil! What triggered this angry outburst? This moment finds Jesus acutely vulnerable. Fearful of what lies ahead, he is determined to stay the course. Perhaps he looks to his friends for support in this risky venture, only to have Peter question his decision. Jesus' anger flares, helping him resist this tempting alternative and keeping him on his difficult course.

As the time of his suffering draws closer, we see Jesus again with his friends—now at prayer in a garden. Here other emotions assault him: anxiety and fear. We are told that he asked to avoid what seemed to lie ahead: "Father, if you are willing, remove this cup from me; yet not my will, but yours be done" (Lk 22:42). For a moment he felt strengthened by an angel, but then the anxiety thickened: "in his anguish he prayed more earnestly, and his sweat became like great drops of blood falling down on the ground" (Lk 22:44). In the midst of this distress Jesus somehow gathers his strength, awakens his dozing friends and prepares to face his fate.

And so further suffering, torture and crucifixion followed. Mark's account in the earliest Gospel recalls that as Jesus hung dying on the cross, he cried out, "My God, my God, why have you abandoned me?" (Mk 15:34). A horrible feeling of desolation struck Jesus at this final hour. Luke's Gospel, written decades later, offers further reflection on the last moments of Jesus' life: "'Father, into your hands I commend my spirit.' Having said this, he breathed his last" (Lk 23:46). In the arc of Jesus' final weeks—from anger, through anxiety and fear and even a moment of searing loneliness—the virtue of courage emerges in the midst of severe emotional distress.

Courage: How We Hold Our Fear

Fear would have us flee every threat to our well-being, to back away from these demands. But courage emboldens us to hold our fear in abeyance, acknowledging our anxiety but not being overcome by it. Josef Pieper, in his account of courage in the theology of Thomas Aquinas, reminds us that the essence of courage "lies not in knowing no fear, but in not allowing oneself to be forced into evil by fear, or to be kept by fear from the realization of good." It is fitting that we are fearful as we face a threatening task, and it is fitting that we go forward at the risk of our own comfort and safety. Fear is not banished but held with respect. Lee Yearley writes, "Courage, then, consists in having a character that lets neither fear nor [too much] confidence unduly change behavior." Conscious of personal vulnerability, the courageous person still goes forward—for the sake of the values involved.

"Do not be afraid"—this encouragement is repeated throughout the Gospels. But there is in our experience much to fear. The world we inhabit today is truly dangerous. Suicide bombers, ethnic cleansing, domestic violence, epidemic disease—there is no lack of reasons to be terrified. We recognize many faces of fear. Anxiety can unravel our plans and unsettle our lives. For some of us, worry can be truly toxic, absorbing our attention so that we cannot move forward. For others, worry triggers planning; we learn that facing this challenging situation will in fact dissolve some of our concern.

Mature courage does not require fearlessness; in fact, courage assumes our vulnerability and strengthens us for action in the face of our fear. "The courageous person is as undaunted as a human being can be," Aristotle insists. But he warns us, "It is not courage to rush impulsively into danger." Some show great bravado but are not genuinely courageous; they are only spoiling for a fight.

The emotional arousal of courage is sometimes subtle. Unlike the emergency emotions of fear or anger, courage is not always accompanied by a physiological surge. We experience the arousal of courage when we are "en-couraged," that is, *en-heartened*. At the conclusion of the story of the disciples returning to Emmaus saddened and afraid, they are excited by the recognition of the stranger as Christ: "Were not our hearts burning within us?" (Lk 24:32). This is, literally, an example of encouragement; they were *enheartened* by the presence of the risen Lord.

Tempering Our Anger

Courage often rides the energy of anger. When those in our care are threatened or values we cherish are at risk, anger often provokes us to their defense. The most universal example is parents who spontaneously—and courageously—struggle against any adversary to protect their children. And anger makes an indispensable contribution when it fuels the courageous pursuit of justice.

Courage is not always laced with anger. One person quietly and courageously faces terminal illness; another confronts a difficult career decision with steady resolve. But anger often erupts in raw, unruly ways. The witness of the prophets' rage, the images of an angry Jesus—these biblical portraits show us that anger is more than moral failure. But honing anger's arousal to support courageous action remains a significant challenge. Paul, in his advice to the Christians in Ephesus, reiterated the advice of the Psalmist: "Be angry and do not sin" (Eph 4:27). This discipline becomes possible as we learn to temper our anger.

For many Americans today, the word *temperance* suggests mildness, reticence and an absence of passion. Christian piety shares some of the blame here, insinuating that truly virtuous persons should absent themselves from passionate behavior. But such a conviction drains temperance of all vitality and distances it from the energetic virtue of courage.

In its truest guise temperance serves as a companion of courage. The one virtue emboldens us to act, while the other moderates our self-expression. When we are angry, we must become sufficiently aroused to resist threat and injustice—without giving in to violence. The metaphor of heat helps us appreciate the contribution of temperance here. Anger heats us up; we get *steamed* as our emotions threaten to boil over in hostile actions. We are in danger of losing our temper. Temperance helps cool the temperature, bringing our arousal down to a productive range. In metallurgy, *to temper* means to refine metal until it is both strong and flexible. A well-tempered piece of steel suits both a war zone and a construction site. Our well-tempered anger both protects and builds up.

Lee Yearley comments on the necessity and danger of anger's contribution to courage. "The passion [of anger] can generate the added impetus that allows a person to overcome fear or some other difficulty," but "a passion like anger easily can slip into powerful and irrational forms. Anger therefore will be a potentially dangerous and always ambivalent part of courageous action."

Courage and temperance are not simply personal resources that we conjure out of individual effort; they are social strengths that are cultivated in supportive communities and in enabling institutions. Ideally, we learn to temper our anger by observing the mature behavior of our parents and colleagues, by participating in conscientious efforts of political action and social reform. In these protected spaces we learn, too, how to moderate our fear.

Courage and Human Flourishing

Courage supports the mature realization that there are values that outweigh our own comfort and security. Aquinas judged that the arousal of courage empowers us "to face the dreadful," strengthening individuals "so that they will not turn back." We feel this arousal when, in the face of a frightening situation, a threat to our safety or our dignity, we determine to act nevertheless. It is not easy to isolate and name this stirring. Reflecting on his child's educational future encourages the parent to raise his voice in opposition at a meeting of the school board. Hoping to guarantee greater economic security for her employees, a business owner makes a risky financial decision. Sometimes we are surprised by our own courageous actions. When asked for an explanation, the best we can offer is: "I just had to do it. I knew I wouldn't be able to live with myself if I didn't."

This broadens our understanding of human flourishing. A full and satisfying life must be open to such risky actions. Courage here often takes the shape of patience. In patience we hold ourselves to valued ideals—of justice, of mercy, of compassion—even when we cannot guarantee that they will win the day. Ultimately, this patience is rooted not in our own effectiveness but in the confident hope that God will prevail.

Jesus offers us this assurance: "I have come so they may have life, and have it in abundance" (Jn 10:10). We are meant to flourish. Our personal safety and happiness are worthy goals. But the instinct for survival is matched by the recognition of values that outweigh personal well-being, values more important than life itself.

Chinese philosopher Mencius recognized this dilemma. "I love life, but there are things I love more than life. That is why I do not cling to life at all costs. I hate death, but there are things I hate more than death. That is why there are some dangers I do not avoid." Martha Nussbaum reminds us of the risks of holding such values. "Courage involves acting against a very appropriate attachment to one's own life, and in that sense, courage has tragedy built into it." And Yearley adds, "Courageous people . . . believe their own safety, or even ordinary happiness, has only a measure of importance."

Sometimes the instinct for personal safety and survival short circuits our courageous impulse. Caution, too well learned, extinguishes courage. Caution warns us not to risk personal disappointment or any disfavor in the eyes of others. Becoming overly cautious, we build a shield around us to protect us from harm but often it instead seals us within our narrow selves. In the end, caution defeats both curiosity and courage.

We can become so attached to our own well-being that we refuse to risk any endeavor that threatens or discomforts us. So we shrink from confrontation and withdraw from challenge. Clinging to our life, we lose all the things that make it valuable. So it may be that for humans, courage is not simply an option—it is a necessary resource for a life well lived.

The Evolution of Quiet Courage

The early cultural image of courage was the warrior. A tribe survived because some members were willing to risk their lives for the community. A nation endured by rewarding bravery among its military forces. In his reflection on courage Aquinas suggests that this rudimentary courage of the warrior has been modified in the course of human history. The heroic bravery-in-battle paradigm has evolved into more sophisticated responses to the subtle threats that persist in society, well beyond bombed buildings and battlefields. In most people's lives today courage is expressed less in attack than in endurance. Theirs is not the heroism of risking life and limb in warfare or police duty, but rather, for example, quietly companioning a loved one through the many months of a lingering illness.

Aquinas insists that remaining faithful in our vocations of love and work requires courage's companion virtue—patience. In seasons of distress and suffering, patience strengthens us so that we do not lose hope, so that we are not made "inordinately sorrowful" by the difficulties we face. In Yearley's account "courage underlies the detachment crucial to survival in bad times."

In a world of conflicting values, a world inhabited by vulnerable people, sadness is a fitting emotion. In our pursuit of high ideals and worthy goals, regret and disappointment are unavoidable. In such a world patience helps us survive our sadness. Patience allows us to honor our losses without being defeated by them. In Pieper's summary of Aquinas's thought he writes, "Patience keeps man from the danger that his spirit may be broken by grief and lose its greatness."

A Christian view of the world, Aquinas insists, will recognize sadness as a true and appropriate emotion: "The world rarely satisfies those who pursue natural justice." We must expect delays and defeats in the pursuit of high ideals. And it is precisely patience-as-endurance that both honors and controls this inevitable sadness. We are sobered by the difficulties that accumulate in any long-term endeavor, but we do not despair.

For Aquinas, patience introduces a religious nuance to courage. Here courage rests on conviction that our efforts are folded into a drama that extends beyond our brief and fragile life. Religious faith awakens us to this larger story and its expansive claim: the coming of the reign of God. This awareness induces in us a mood of peace in the face of life's trials. Aquinas identifies this tranquility as a gift of the Holy Spirit.

Courage and Hope

The virtue of courage is ultimately rooted in hope, "an expectation that safety is close at hand." Hope begins in expectant desire. This future orientation is often accompanied by discomfort with how things are now. And hope's arousal motivates action, encouraging us to move toward this promising future. So hope encompasses more than an immediate emotional arousal; mature hope functions as a reliable psychological strength and a resilient social resource.

Erik Erikson has made a major contribution to our understanding of hope. Hope is a psychological strength, emerging initially in infants and maturing into an essential characteristic or virtue in adult life. "Hope is an enduring belief in the attainability of fervent wishes, in spite of the dark urges and rages which mark the beginning of existence." Erikson argues, "Hope is both the earliest and the most indispensable virtue inherent in the state of being alive." The foundations of hope are laid in the early exchanges between infants and their caring parents. Again, Erikson writes: "The infant's smile inspires hope in the adult and, in making him smile, makes him wish to give hope." Through this mutual interaction a child grows in confidence that the world is trustworthy—here my needs will be recognized, honored, and (often) satisfied. Our capacity for hope grows out of and is nourished by these early experiences of trust.

Social psychology, focused on the interaction between self and society, sees hope as a critical foundation of social action. Our capacity for hope influences how we embrace our own life and how we contribute to the larger world. Psychologist C. R. Snyder has pioneered this analysis of the hope as a social resource. For Snyder, hopeful people develop two important strategies: *pathways thinking*—setting concrete objectives and envisioning ways these might be achieved; and *agency thinking*—devising practical strategies to move along these pathways toward the desired goals. Hopeful people, then, have goals to which they aspire. They believe in their ability to find ways to meet these goals, and they actually follow through toward successful completion.

Victoria McGeer expands the scope of hope's contribution to effective social change. For McGeer, hope involves more than an awareness of the difficulty that confronts us "out there." Hope sustains us in situations where our own resources—talent or strength or influence—are limited. But rather than simply giving up, hope encourages us to persevere. Thus hope provides energy and direction toward the goal of a better world and also toward expanding our resources to help build that better world. Moving beyond its initial emotional arousal, then, hope becomes a reliable resource in support of transformation.

McGeer identifies characteristics of those for whom hope has become a reliable strength. When obstacles are put in their way, hopeful people become even more determined. They adapt more easily to unexpected circumstances; when one door closes they look for another to open. In this way those who hope well often discover untapped resources in the midst of the difficult situation. Fresh alternatives for action seem to present themselves, and new personal strengths may emerge.

This mature hope strengthens commitment. In McGeer's words:

> Although there may be nothing we can do now to bring about what we desire, our energy is still oriented toward the future, limitations notwithstanding. Our interest, our concern, our desires, our passions—all of these continue to be engaged by what can be; hence, we lean into the future ready to act when actions can do some good.

Maturing in hope does not always demand that the world satisfy our demands. Hope for a particular outcome may be dashed. But when this disappointment occurs, those who hope well are able to retain their commitment as they explore other possibilities for action.

Learning to Hope Well

The capacity to hope seems to come partly as a gift. Psychologists recognize many factors that are involved—family upbringing and social circumstances and even genetic makeup. But being able to hope well is also a skill that can be developed over time. How do we develop our capacity for mature hope? The simple answer: by hanging out with the hopeful! Mobilizing hope as a resource for social transformation depends to considerable extent on being in touch with the hopes of other people.

Continuing to hope in the face of the resistant obstacles to change depends on finding a community of people sustained by mutual support. In these emotionally responsive groups our own commitments are strengthened as we reinforce one another's hopeful energy. Communities of hope maintain a sense of efficacy, of agency, of confidence in their capacity to cope with difficulties ahead. Motivation is sustained by our openness to one another's concerns. Their hopes and our hopes become linked.

Especially when our efforts are focused on social transformation, remaining hopeful can depend on a network of other hopeful people. This mutual support does not mean that we must endorse everything that our partners in social change promote. Sometimes we have to challenge those with whom we share significant commitments: questioning current strategies, urging clearer understanding of our common objectives, proposing different pathways toward our shared goals. But we sustain our hopes best in the company of responsive others.

Honoring Religious Hope

For many involved today in movements of social transformation, hope is rooted in faith in God. Religious hope is not simply a conviction that certain objectives will occur. Rather, it is a confidence that ultimately God will prevail. This trust in God does not overlook the need for personal courage or the hard work of social reform. But faith supplies an additional resource in support of these ongoing efforts. Among religiously sensitive people hope in God sustains our practical efforts, nurtures our commitment to seek out alternate pathways and motivates our continued action even in the face of delay or defeat.

Here faith is the predisposition of hope. The hope that is the ground of courage lifts us out of a narrow self-concern and centers our attention on God. Recognizing that we are part of a reality greater than ourselves alone, we are set free to invest our lives in hopes that will outlive us. We are now free even to fail in the world's eyes because "there are some things I love more than life."

We recall the gospel account in which Jesus invites his disciples to "set out into the deep" (Lk 5:4). The "deep" is unknown territory, filled with risk, hinting at dangers of drowning and shipwreck. To "set out into the deep" takes courage; to continue to hug the shore cautiously will not do. So, in trepidation and hope, and in league with hopeful others, we set out into deeper waters.

Courage serves as a healing emotion. When we confront injustice or indifference, the arousal of courage heals the fear and anger that would weaken our response. Courage welcomes hope—the hope that predicts, even against present evidence, a better future. In the face of a world that does not support our deepest desires, courage engenders patience and even faith in God's ultimate triumph. In all these ways courage heals and strengthens our fragile hearts.

5

Curiosity and Contentment

Taking the day off, I treat myself to an afternoon exploring the museum's new exhibit. I wander from room to room until I come across a painting that captures my attention. There I stand rooted in place, not even sure why this particular work appeals to me so strongly. While other patrons pass by, speaking softly, I search out a place to sit so that I can spend more time here. What is the artist attempting? Why is her vision so compelling for me? No clear answers come, as I remain seated—entranced—for some time. Gradually a mood of calm envelops me, with feelings of ease and contentment. I am grateful—for this setting, for this day, and for more.

A Family of Emotions

Feelings often cluster in families. The positive emotions of interest, curiosity, appreciation and contentment share a genetic line. Here we trace their connections, tracking the movement of interest and curiosity toward feelings of appreciation and the subsequent mood of contentment.

Interest has been identified as "thinking with excitement." The arousal of interest carries us beyond a narrow self-focus to engage with broader aspects of our experience. This positive emotion rescues us from our solitude, expands our attention and may even recruit our care for others. Lacking interest in something or someone, we often respond dismissively, "I just don't care." Barbara Fredrickson observes that "Interest animates and enlivens the mind" by focusing attention and mobilizing us for engagement and interaction. She adds, "interest is the primary instigator of personal growth, creative endeavor, and development of intelligence." Drawing us out of isolation, sustained interest expands our store of knowledge and enhances our cognitive abilities. Even as interest stimulates exploratory behavior, the lack of this expansive energy often strands us in boredom.

Passionate Curiosity

While interest names the initial arousal that focuses our attention, curiosity identifies the energy that impels us to make contact. Early in a child's life curiosity surfaces as a raw enthusiasm. Through their instruction and their modeling behavior parents hope to shape and direct this vital energy. In puberty curiosity draws our attention to physical changes and sexual arousals. The impulse of curiosity leads the adolescent out of self-absorption toward both friendship and sexual experimentation. And the fascination of teenage romance—for all its perils—can develop psychological strengths that prepare us for the life-long commitments of love and mature devotion.

Curiosity's energy also fuels the search for a satisfying adult identity. Shall I become a teacher or a musician, a police officer or a scientist? Will marriage and family life be part of my own future? Curiosity lures us to take those tentative steps that may lead to a satisfying life and fruitful career. With proper cultivation this vital energy accompanies us through adult life as a well-honed resource.

Jodi Halpern, a medical doctor and therapist studying "engaged curiosity," is convinced that a well-cultivated curiosity in the therapist evokes curiosity in the patient, thereby enabling the person to examine his or her own condition more reflectively. Such curiosity also helps the therapist avoid stereotyping patients and their conditions.

In a recent survey of business leaders Nell Minow, co-founder of the Corporate Library, names "passionate curiosity" as the quality looked for in major hiring decisions. Some people may be passionate, but their interest is often focused on a single objective; others are curious, but they are content to watch passively as the world goes by. Minow gives priority to "somebody who is just alert and very awake and engaged with the world and wanting to know more."

Curiosity as a Vice

Curiosity's enthusiastic desire comes under attack both early in the Christian tradition and in contemporary life. Writing in the fourth century the authoritative Christian thinker Jerome inveighed against this eagerness for knowledge. Thomas Aquinas quotes Jerome: "Is it not evident that a man who day and night wrestles with the dialectic art, the student of natural science whose gaze pierces the heavens, walks in vanity of understanding and darkness of mind?"

For Jerome, curiosity was a kind of pride—an unrestrained desire to understand the workings of the world. So he condemned curiosity as inappropriate interest. In his view, curiosity's unrestrained energy turned its desire to know into a kind of lust. Thus a double indictment: curiosity as fueled by both pride and lust.

Augustine, writing in his memoir *The Confessions,* appears to share this judgment. Prominent among the unholy desires that plagued his youth was curiosity: "my ears tickled with false stories so they would itch all the more with curiosity" (1:10). Near the end of this account Augustine includes curiosity in the list of the distractions that still beset him. Lust—the disordered seeking of every kind of pleasure— finds expression not only in sexual temptations but also in surges of curiosity, which Augustine interprets as "vain" and "morbid" (10:35). Augustine was not able to appreciate that his personal fascination with theological issues—the workings of memory, the efficacy of grace— arose from his passionate curiosity.

Eight hundred years later Thomas Aquinas examined this question of curiosity as a vice. Aquinas was aware that his own intellectual quest was fueled by passionate interest, much like the energy condemned by Jerome and Augustine. Influenced by Aristotle's more optimistic understanding of humanity's desire to know, Aquinas offered a distinction. Healthy curiosity he named *studiositas,* the focused drive that keeps the scientist in the laboratory late into the night. This potentially virtuous form of curiosity was opposed to the promiscuous lust for information, *curiositas.*

Social critics today find much evidence of the latter kind of obsessive curiosity. The "up to the minute" news cycle on radio and television, the popularity of gossip and "tell-all" journalism, the celebrity-chasing frenzy of much media reporting—these excesses infect our cultural life. Paul Griffiths rails against this cultural abuse: "Late modern societies that are fundamentally shaped by the overwhelming presence of electronic media and the obscene inundation of every aspect of human life by pictures and sounds have turned *the vice of curiosity* into a prescribed way of life." Griffiths may also have in mind the familiar scene of individuals checking their email accounts and Facebook sites repeatedly throughout the day.

Griffiths lists the cultural imperatives that support these excesses: follow the inquiry as far as it goes, leave no stone unturned, there is always more to know, the more information the better. "In a world where curiosity rules," Griffiths declares, "unmasking curiosity as a destructive and offensive device . . . amounts to nothing less than a . . . radical critique of superficiality and constant distraction."

Just as Aquinas chose to distinguish the healthy impulse of *studiositas* from the unrestrained and compulsive force of *curiositas,* we may observe examples today where this inquisitive drive to know—so unfocused in infancy and childhood—has been channeled in adult life into a dedicated pursuit of important goals. But equally, this energy can remain distracted and unfocused. Here *idle curiosity* moves promiscuously from interest to interest, arousal to arousal. We sample life widely but find no place to dwell; nothing "captures our attention" in ways that support the risks of lasting commitment or long-term engagement. Idle curiosity—*curiositas*—finds little satisfaction and bears no fruit.

Voyeurism is another face of idle curiosity. Watching from a distance, the voyeur remains safe from risk, unengaged. In U.S. culture today, celebrity-watching is a major preoccupation; one need only witness the sensational headlines of the tabloid newspapers stacked at supermarket check-out counters. Gossip and rumor feed on a diet of idle curiosity. Barbara Benedict defines gossip as "an unregulated exchange of unverified information that commodifies others." Around the water cooler we trade stories of the downfall of authorities or the indiscretions of colleagues. We relish exchanging these rumors. While these distractions may pique our curiosity, this information does not enlighten and does not heal.

Pornography is a graphic example of a curiosity "idling" in unhealthy distractions. Pornography provides arousals that are disconnected from both respect and enduring contact. And because this pseudo-intimacy does not satisfy, we find ourselves seeking this stimulation again and again, hoping—in Augustine's famous phrase—"to satisfy the insatiable." As this repetitive behavior becomes addictive, stimulation continues but finds no contentment.

Curiosity can be wounded in other ways as well. In a sheltering family setting the children may be constantly warned of dangers abiding in the world "out there." These early messages, taken to heart, may leave them overly cautious. They learn to abide by the rules and hold outsiders at a safe distance. Soon caution displaces curiosity. Humorist Garrison Keillor indicts his Christian upbringing for instilling this kind of crippling caution: "You taught me the fear of becoming lost, which has killed the pleasure of curiosity and discovery. In strange cities, I memorize streets and always know exactly where I am. Amid scenes of great splendor, I review the route back to the hotel."

Appreciation as an Emotional Embrace

Someone or something catches our eye; we are attracted by loveliness or charm. We turn from our busy life to pay attention—to admire and to savor. Consider the peculiar pleasure experienced as our eyes move over a field of wildflowers. Their color, profusion and delicate movement in the breeze arouse our delight. As we gaze at them, an appreciation arises within us that does not aspire to be quickly sated. We linger over this pleasure, savoring rather than quenching it. The mood accompanying the pleasure of appreciation is not relief but gratitude. Feeling this delight, we are taken out of ourselves. Until that moment we may have been distracted or sad, but under the influence of this pleasure our self-absorption dissipates and a different mood settles in.

Appreciation signals a special kind of knowing and a distinct style of intimacy. When we savor a melody or taste, we come to know it in an intimate fashion (the word *savor* is related to the French word *savoir*, meaning "to know"). Savoring also suggests the appreciation that is part of physical taste. We find our delight in the delicious. Fast food, quickly consumed, seldom offers this kind of experience. In savoring something our enjoyment lingers—taking time to appreciate the subtle flavors in food, the changing colors of a sunset or the contours of our lover's face.

When we are thirsty, a drink of cold water quickly satisfies. And we announce our appreciation in the past tense: "That was good!" The thirst is finished; life goes on. But as we savor a glass of fine wine or a selection of music that we love, our appreciation dwells in the present. Instead of "That was good," our delight dwells in the present tense: "This is good."

In *Savor: Mindful Eating, Mindful Life* the Buddhist practice of mindfulness is linked with the enjoyment of food. Through the practice of mindful eating, we heighten our appreciation. Mindful eating entails taking time, allowing ourselves to experience each taste and texture. A decision to savor our food suggests eating small portions of healthy food slowly and with gratefulness. Because this practice of attentive consumption often increases our awareness of those who go without food, mindful eating can makes us both more appreciative and more compassionate.

The authors, Thich Nhat Hanh and Lilian Cheung, describe a communal meal prepared with a Buddhist cook. Those who gathered at the table were encouraged to begin the meal by taking a piece of the freshly baked bread. Before tasting, they were asked to smile—with gratitude—at the bread in their hands as a way of acknowledging the human effort involved in the grain production and the baking process. Only then were they encouraged to take a bite, "chewing and tasting only the bread, and not the worries in our minds."

The practice of mindful eating overcomes the tendency to eat "on the run" with little attention to what we are ingesting. Eating in this way has little in common with the dominant pattern at many U.S. tables—conspicuous consumption of large portions of rich but unhealthy food. In mindful eating body and mind come together; both are involved in simple actions of nourishment and gratitude.

Appreciating Beauty

Beauty—in sight or sound or even in memory—grabs our attention. We stop what we had been doing, so that we may be more aware of what is before us now. "The startling and sometimes overwhelming encounter with beauty opens up something essential in the human heart, drawing us out of ourselves and inviting us to an engagement with the transcendent." Patrick McCormick continues, "Beauty does not merely please and attract us, it also derails and releases us from obsessive and deadly attention to the self or the routines of survival."

Elaine Scarry observes that this *arresting* quality of beauty brings together aesthetics and ethics. When we notice the fragility of an antique vase or the delicate loveliness of a small child, we become more attentive, more respectful. "Noticing its beauty increases the possibility that it will be carefully handled." While beautiful items are good simply in themselves, they may also serve a larger purpose for our busy lives. Beholding something beautiful we are drawn away from distractions of the day into a more generous presence to the world, spurring, Scarry notes, our "lapsed alertness back to its more acute level."

To *appreciate* carries overtones of both value and gratitude. When we truly appreciate other people, we are likely to give thanks, to them and to God, for their presence in our lives. And as appreciation grows—for the many contributions of a senior colleague or a dedicated professional or a generous donor—we seek ways to honor them as a demonstration of our respect. In these acts of appreciation we both acknowledge their dignity and expand its scope. Appreciating others for their own sake reinforces feelings of contentment and satisfaction within them and within us as well.

The Mood of Contentment

I have learned to be content with whatever I have . . . I have been paid in full and have more than enough; I am fully satisfied.

—PHILIPPIANS 4:11

Contentment initiates a particular frame of mind—the delight of resting, of *basking*—in appreciation of "what is now." We have seen that curiosity opens us to a wider appreciation of our world, and interest supports productive engagement with the delights and problems of this world. This energetic involvement often bears fruit in feelings of contentment. We might trace this as the arc of appreciation: from the initial arousal of curiosity through a sustained exercise of appreciative engagement to a conclusion in a mood of contentment. This mood—part delight and part relief—often arises at the conclusion of some significant work. In contentment there is no need to gloat; we need not calculate margins of victory. Instead, we simply savor what has been brought to life. In Barbara Fredrickson's judgment "this emotion prompts individuals to savor the moment or recent experiences, feel *oneness* with others or the world around them, and integrate current and recent experiences into their overall self-concept and world view."

For Fredrickson, contentment enhances our life as it "serves to encourage integration of self with environment, thus expanding our view of the world." In these ways contentment broadens and builds our resources. Contentment carves out time to focus on the blessings we have received, and supports our readiness to give thanks.

In *Virtuous Passions* Simon Harak explores ways that joy and delight continue to echo in the mood of contentment. These feelings arise when we reach a chosen goal; they register a fulfillment of desire. Aquinas, Harak reminds us, finds another emotion evoked by satisfied desire: the experience of *quies* or "rest." For Thomas, the motivating passion of desire leads us to both delight and contentment *(quies)*.

Feeling content is similar to feeling satisfied. Both emotions encourage us to interrupt our busy schedules so that we might take pleasure in what has just transpired. *Satisfaction* adds to contentment a judgment of *enough* (*satis* in Latin). We know the satisfaction that comes with a job well done or from a difficult task that we have managed to complete—even against the odds. An interior instinct alerts us here: now it is time to slow down, to acknowledge what has been achieved, to relish this sense of completion before the demands of the rest of our life rush in.

Still, questions may arise: When is enough *enough*? How can we be confident that our current resources—of time or money, of social achievement or public recognition—are sufficient? The moral maxim—*zhi zu* or "know when enough is enough"—is deeply ingrained in the Chinese culture. This phrase, celebrated in calligraphy and exemplified in classic literature, remains cherished by Chinese people today, even as the fast-paced environments of Hong Kong, Taiwan and mainland China offer little support to living out its demands.

The Chinese tradition also includes other calls to contentment. Confucian philosopher Mencius saw links between virtuous behavior (following the *Tao*) and *being at ease,* a quality of life that we might call *contentment.* "A virtuous person steeps himself in the *Tao* because he wishes to find it in himself. When he finds it in himself, he will be at ease in it; when he is at ease in it, he will draw deeply on it; when he can draw deeply on it, he finds its source wherever he turns."

Augustine, plagued by an addictive personality, recognized that his own constant search for pleasure could never bring him true satisfaction. He recalls the moral chaos that marked his youth, when he was driven by a profligate desire for sex and worldly honors. He reports the continuing struggle to transform this chronic restlessness into an enduring search for God. His memoir concludes with a prayer to God who is "forever at rest."

The comforting mood of contentment, cousin to serenity and tranquility, remains elusive in our world. Distracted throughout the day by multiple obligations, we sense we have little time to rest. Too many tasks remain untended. In a culture that extols hard work, increased production and steady achievement, contentment is considered an unaffordable luxury.

Contentment in a Consumer Economy

A consumer economy does not thrive on contentment. A nation's economic growth depends on sustaining and expanding the purchasing patterns of its citizens. People who are discontent with what they have now become ideal consumers. Mary Jo Leddy describes this as "culturally induced dissatisfaction." Ethicist William Schweiker comments, "In a consumer, media-driven culture, where our desires are constantly being stimulated, saturated by social values, we face a deep dilemma indeed . . . Can we really forsake trying to understand and transform the forces that are shaping our world and our lives?"

Encouraged to fasten our attention on celebrities and the wealthy, we become like children with noses pressed against the storefront window, admiring what we do not have. We are instructed in the inadequacy of our own small lives. All this engenders regret, resentment and envy—each an enemy of contentment.

At the heart of a consuming culture lies a cruel parody of spiritual aspiration. The spiritual quest is rooted in the desire for something *more* in life—more than the monotonous daily grind of work, eat, sleep, work. Augustine wrote eloquently of the spiritual life as one of restlessness: "Our hearts are restless until they rest in Thee." A consuming culture promises more—new fashions, novel products, upgraded gadgets. Our current culture also instills in us a restlessness. Here our yearning gets redirected to improvements in status that we hope might someday afford some satisfaction. Tom Beaudoin describes this peculiar parody: "The human ability to desire more, which drives us to transcendence, can turn into a fruitless quest for fulfillment through acquisition of ever more temporal goods."

A humble step toward healing this cultural malaise may lie in giving attention to what Michael Leunig calls our "noble tiredness." In a consuming society we had been trained to be always on the move, ever on the alert. Multi-tasking as we go, we keep moving forward, regretting the demeaning limits imposed by our daily fatigue. The sleep deprivation, poor eating habits and stress that ensue guarantee the absence of any lasting contentment. Perhaps our rejection of this exhausting treadmill lies in learning to honor our tiredness. In the lovely parables of his *Curly Pyjama Letters*, Leunig writes: "Tiredness is one of our strongest, most noble and instructive feelings . . . It is an important aspect of our conscience and must be heeded or else we will not survive." He continues, "When you are tired—you must rest like the trees and animals do . . . and enjoyment will surely follow." In such honoring of our vulnerability, we may be surprised by stirrings of contentment long absent from our lives.

Each of the emotional states we have discussed here—curiosity, appreciation, contentment—is available to us, free of charge. But each is subject to distractions that can undermine it. If we allow this to happen, these natural gifts are squandered. Here too we recognize the challenges of a spirituality of the healing emotions. As we become more able to tune our days to the rhythms of curiosity, appreciation and contentment, our lives expand and we become more fully alive.

PART II

HEALING EMOTIONS

Healing emotions name those feelings that await healing, but also surges of affection, compassion and pride that bring about a healing of the heart.

Joy appears throughout the Gospels, registering the presence of the Spirit and the arrival of grace.

Attachment names emotional bonds that link us with our companions and with our God, bonds we cannot do without.

The emotion of pride, a judgment of excellence and worth, celebrates delights and successes, large and small, reminding us we are made for great things.

The body-based emotion of compassion expands into the virtue that resides at the heart of Christian life.

Christians have long been hesitant toward powerful emotions; this uncertainty is charted in the mood swings in the life of faith.

6

Joy and Happiness

*This is the day the Lord has made; let us rejoice
and be glad.*

—Psalm 118:24

Emotions, as we have seen, often gather comfortably into families. Joy, happiness, delight and laughter are linked in this way. These emotions frame our experiences of celebration, jubilation, even exaltation—encounters that call forth an alleluia. While these feelings themselves may not function well as ultimate goals, they serve us as guidelines, alerting us that we are on the right path.

Happiness and joy appear high on everyone's list of positive feelings. Sometimes the words are used interchangeably. And often these feelings overlap in our experience. But recognizing the particular quality of each of these arousals provides richer insight into our emotional lives. For example, joy corresponds more closely to the model of a *discrete emotion*, since it includes an identifiable pattern of physiological arousal and a somewhat focused—and time-limited—response. Happiness is a more complex experience—a state of mind that extends over some period of time, usually includes a range of emotions and involves a higher degree of cognitive activity. We begin here with a focus on joy, returning to happiness later in the chapter.

Researchers take a wide focus in their examination of joy. Language itself expands the possibilities: we enjoy and rejoice; we are joyful and joyous; we may even become overjoyed. These feelings arise as we relish and take pleasure in our lives. Laughter and smiles, humor and delight—these, too, are familiar manifestations of joy. And this emotion may be the only feeling to have its own assassin—killjoy.

Most of us recognize the expressions of joy as positive feelings. The arousals are pleasant in our here-and-now experience. So we welcome these feelings for their own sake, not just in terms of later benefits they bring or further goals they support. But even if these emotions are not goal oriented, they have reliable outcomes. Feelings of delight, for example, support the urge to play, to test the limits. This arousal promotes creativity and skills acquisition. We are more likely to stay involved in activities that we enjoy, so we more easily acquire competence and confidence in the task at hand.

The family of joy includes our everyday experiences of laughter. Humor responds to incongruity. We laugh in response to unexpected connections and unanticipated events. Comedians use this to their advantage, setting up elaborate scenarios that depend on the audience "getting the joke" as people recognize the surprise ending.

Laughter strengthens our connections with one another. Paul Pahil reminds us that "amusement is social. We can laugh alone but this is pale rendition of laughter we share with others." The ability to make other people laugh—without resorting to derision or mockery—makes a valuable contribution to a group's life. Linking us in a positive emotional response, shared humor signals solidarity. Laughing together, we sense that we are safe among friends.

Joy, too, strengthens our ties with those whose presence we cherish. And, as George Vaillant insists, joy finds profound expression in close relationships—when friendship deepens, when separation is overcome, when devotion is shared, when love is affirmed. Joy lingers even in the face of difficulties; its inner radiance illumines our present experience and brightens moments ahead. "We feel joy when we appreciate life—when we contemplate nature, when we recognize our freedom, and when we dwell on our successful relationships with other people. We feel joy when we have faith in something larger than ourselves." In all these ways joy expands and heals our hearts.

Christian Memories of Joy—Response to the Good News

> *I am bringing you good news of great joy for all the people!*
>
> —LUKE 2:10

In the Christian tradition joy occupies a privileged place as the register of the good news. Savoring that we are born in the image of God, recalling that our failures can be forgiven, sharing in the community of faith—in all these realizations our response is a healing movement of joy. In the New Testament the feeling of joy *(chara)* is closely related to the experience of grace *(charis)*; joy, then, may be a signature emotion marking our encounters with grace.

Luke's Gospel emphasizes what we might call the embodied jolt of joy. When Mary becomes pregnant with Jesus, she travels to visit her cousin Elizabeth, who is also expecting a child. At the sound of Mary's voice Elizabeth experiences a surge of excitement. "The child in my womb leapt with joy" (Lk 1:41). Years later John the Baptist denies that he is the messiah, insisting instead that he is like the friend at the wedding party who "rejoices greatly at the bridegroom's voice." Jesus is the one for whom Israel has been waiting, and "for this reason my joy has been fulfilled" (Jn 3:29).

Throughout the New Testament joy marks the entry of God into our lives—made present through Jesus' healing and the Spirit's energizing appearance. Jesus himself is at times filled with "joy in the Spirit" (Lk 10:21). In the Acts of the Apostles a dizzying joy floods the disciples at Pentecost, as they become aware of God's Spirit in their midst (13:52).

Joy appears regularly in the parables in response to the surprising workings of grace. "The kingdom of heaven is like a treasure hidden in a field, which someone found and hid; then in his joy he goes and sells all that he has and buys that field" (Mt 13:44). When Jesus' disciples witnessed him performing miracles or debating those who challenged him, they "rejoiced at all the glorious things that were done by him" (Lk 13:17).

In these gospel settings joy is more than a "feel good" emotion; its robust arousal coexists with great suffering. A classic example of the interplay appears in John's Gospel, where the pain of childbirth gives way to the joy that a child has been born (Jn 16:20). Here Jesus uses this image to prepare his disciples for the suffering he foresees in his own future, an anguish that will give way to the joy of new life.

At the conclusion of Matthew's Gospel we read of the women who visit the tomb where Jesus had been laid, only to find it empty. They flee the scene, flooded with mixed emotions: "filled with joy and fear" (28:8). In the first letter to the Thessalonians (1:6), Paul recognizes the followers of Jesus who, while suffering severe persecution, remain filled with joy. In his letter to the Galatians (5:22), Paul includes joy among the consolations that signal the presence of the Spirit.

Thomas Aquinas discusses joy as an emotion that marks the culmination of desire. United with a beloved person or reaching a cherished goal, we experience the contentment that Aquinas names delight or joy. Diana Cates, in her commentary on Aquinas's understanding of joy, notes the bodily sensations involved: "a movement that feels like opening, expanding, and being elevated, in a way that is attended by bodily sensations of relaxation, warmth, or increased energy." Cates concludes, "A religious emotion of joy would involve thoughts, intuitions, or questions concerning one's relationship to what lies beyond, beneath, or at the heart of ordinary reality."

Enjoyment was a cause of concern for Augustine. Troubled as he was with the seductive appeal of sensual delights, Augustine judged that enjoyment—the appeal of beautiful sights and sounds and tastes—was more likely to seduce us than lead us to God. This pessimistic view brought him to a stark conclusion: "*God alone may be enjoyed*; creatures may not constitute the final resting place of our hearts and wills, but may only be used as instruments and not as ends in themselves." Augustine proceeds here from a narrow understanding of enjoyment: "To enjoy is to cleave to something for its own sake, in love." This all-consuming experience of loving attachment is fitting only in our relationship with God. To enjoy anything else was seen by Augustine as an illusion, akin even to idolatry.

Happiness as Religious Blessing

You will go out in gladness and be led forth in peace. The mountains and hills will burst into song before you, and all the trees of the field will clap their hands.

—Isaiah 55:12

For much of human history happiness has been celebrated as a received blessing, a gift bestowed rather than a personal achievement. *Baruch*, the term used in the Hebrew bible for happiness, can be translated "blessing." In the New Testament accounts of Jesus' Sermon on the Mount, the Greek term *makarios* designates both happiness and blessing: "Happy are those who hunger and thirst for justice, for they shall be filled." In the biblical tradition to count one's blessings is to trace the mysterious route to authentic happiness. We are happy *because* we have received God's blessing.

An earlier generation of Catholics learned as children that eternal happiness was their destiny. The catechism opens with the question: "Why did God make you?" The answer: "To know, love and serve

God in this world and to be happy with Him forever in the next." Life's later lessons would add nuance to this original insight. But from the start, happiness was recognized as both a blessing and a birthright.

In addition, the readings and rituals of the liturgical year alert the community of faith to positive emotions. The advent season leading up to the celebration of Jesus' birth evokes feelings of anticipation, a barely restrained delight that includes thoughts of holiday decorations, special foods and anticipated gifts. And in the appointed prayers for the Third Sunday of Advent we hear the explicit call: "Rejoice. Again, I tell you rejoice!" (Phil 4:4).

As the year wears on, the season of Lent approaches with its sober mood: Ash Wednesday, followed by six weeks of prayer and fasting. But here too the church calendar incorporates a strategic pause. Laetare ("rejoice") Sunday, falling in the midst of this penitential period, proclaims the words of Isaiah: "Rejoice, Jerusalem! (Is 66:10). In the somber days of Holy Week that follow, the community gathers to remember Jesus' passion, with its emotions of grief and lamentation. Then more cause for rejoicing, as Easter bursts forth in celebrations of color and chorus. Happiness is again our birthright, bestowed.

Yet many of us remain hesitant about the place of happiness in a life of faith. Echoing Augustine, we recognize that we live with original sin behind us, the threat of eternal punishment ahead, and temptations present all around. Any current distress must be borne in the hope of the happiness that awaits us after death.

Modern Perspectives on Happiness

As modern consciousness dawned among intellectuals in eighteenth-century Europe, new perspectives on happiness began to emerge. Suffering was disentangled from sin. Increasingly the sources of the world's distress were seen to lie neither in planetary movements nor in God's inscrutable design, but in human injustice. A concerted effort to reduce ignorance, illness and greed in human society would, political thinkers confidently predicted, create conditions of greater happiness for all.

Buoyed by a new confidence in science as the source of progress and convinced that political reform would soon improve society, intellectuals and activists argued that humanity was designed for happiness. From this new confidence arose an understanding of "life, liberty and the pursuit of happiness" as essential components of the good life, properly available to all citizens of the modern political state. Happiness thus became an essential birthright of human nature, no longer a blessing dependent on the gracious response of God or the monarch of the realm.

In today's world we have become accustomed to the understanding that happiness is a state of mind—even an emotion—to which we are entitled. We are aggrieved when conditions, whether a sluggish economy or natural disaster or other misfortune, block our access to this mood. But soon we come to the sober realization that even if the pursuit of happiness is guaranteed, its actual possession remains difficult.

Lessons about happiness come, too, from paradox. A friend loses a long-held job and then discovers another career focus that, to his amazement, brings satisfaction and delight. Another person, surviving cancer surgery or an automobile accident, experiences newfound happiness in the simple pleasures of being alive—sources of enjoyment she had previously overlooked. Here again happiness comes more as blessing than an achievement.

The Positive Psychology of Happiness

Happiness, like joy, supports healing. Psychologists recognize happiness as less a single identifiable emotion and more an experienced mood or even a state of consciousness. Happiness exists in direct awareness; we *know* when we are happy. As we come to this awareness, the testimony of our own experience counts most. Feelings of happiness often respond to *hedonic* factors—physical pleasure, comfortable surroundings, enjoyable activities. But happiness also responds to *eudaimonic* factors—rooted in experiences of life satisfaction and personal meaning that go beyond physical delight.

While most of us recognize the pleasant arousals of happiness, some people are happier than others. To better understand this difference, psychologists have explored happiness as a character trait or an emotional disposition. Here happiness is about much more than superficial cheerfulness or the bland encouragement to "have a nice day." A person disposed to happiness does not necessarily live a carefree life. An orientation toward happiness does not deny the experience of pain or distress; it does not overlook tragedy in one's own life or in the world. But characteristically happy people draw on a range of positive feelings as they evaluate themselves and events in their lives. Instead of simply turning away or seeking distractions in the face of suffering, people disposed to happiness display a greater readiness to examine their painful experiences more deeply. Often they find life-enhancing elements there, even in the midst of their distress.

In their efforts to describe happiness—practically and experientially—psychologists have identified four contexts that contribute significantly to human flourishing. Physical well-being counts as a significant dimension of emotional satisfaction throughout life. Maintaining the body's inner sense of vitality contributes to both health and psychological well-being. So the pursuit of happiness includes a commitment to care for our body and its particular needs. From those of us who live with disabilities or suffer chronic illness, as well as the rapidly expanding cohort of older Americans, we learn that physical limitations need not be barriers to happiness. Psychologists have identified resources of *responsible renunciation* that support a person's continued happiness and well-being in the face of physical diminishment. Renunciation is real—the need to let go those activities and goals that are no longer available to us. But our self-emptying proceeds responsibly, with efforts to hold on as long as possible, even as we prepare to let go when this is required.

Pleasure and beauty open a second perspective on happiness, delighting our senses and expanding our engagement in world around us. Good food, invigorating activity and sexual delight, pleasing colors and shapes and sounds—these are benefits of our embodiment. Sensual pleasures usually last only a short time. Paying attention, then, is one of the demands of the pleasant life. Physical pleasure passes quickly, but we can honor its fragility through disciplines of timing and pacing. Developing greater mindfulness helps us to be more present to our experience here and now. As we learn to seek out beauty and to linger in delight, sensual pleasure becomes more available as a source of our happiness.

The engaged life provides another orientation to happiness. Here happiness comes as we make use of our own capacities; we delight in doing what we do well. Successful results or outside approval may be appreciated, if these additional benefits come. But the greatest source of happiness is often the work itself. The engaged life moves us beyond the experience of physical pleasure. The tasks that absorb our attention and energy here are often difficult, sometimes even dangerous. But we are engaged in the activity itself as much as in its final goal.

Both psychological literature and the evidence of our own lives testify to another source of happiness—the meaningful life. This orientation widens to include more than pleasure and the full expression of our own talent. A meaningful life may well include the blessings of delight and accomplishment, but its particular contribution to our happiness comes from a deeper source, from the conviction that our life is linked to something more significant than just ourselves. Through our value commitments and life activities, we participate in a richer realm of reality. As Daniel Siegel acknowledges, "The study of positive psychology suggests that being involved in something larger than a personal self creates a sense of meaning and well-being—an essential part of the experience of 'happiness.'"

In a meaningful life the self seeks happiness neither simply in delight (as in the pleasant life), nor chiefly in achievement (as in the engaged life). Happiness here draws on an experience of transcending the self, the realization that we are sustained by and contribute to a broader perspective.

Happiness and pleasure have this in common: if we pursue either of these in isolation, we are likely to be frustrated. Neither happiness nor pleasure can bear the weight of a single-minded pursuit. These rich human experiences flow from other values. Pleasure and happiness arise as we do what we are designed for: love well, keep our promises, honor what is worthy, contribute to the common good. Siegel continues: "We are built to be a 'we'—and enter a more fulfilling state, perhaps a more natural way of being, when we connect in meaningful ways with others." Apart from such endeavors, happiness and pleasure are likely to elude us.

Human Flourishing—More than Happiness

Flourishing is good, nevertheless seeking it is not our highest goal.

—CHARLES TAYLOR

After a century of searching out remedies for the maladies that afflict humankind, psychological researchers have turned their attention to the positive dynamics that guide a satisfying and fruitful life. The new focus of positive psychology puts social scientists again in touch with Aristotle's philosophical discussion of *eudaimonia*, human flourishing. The ancient Greeks identified humanity's quandary: how to link the ideal of rational self-sufficiency with the unavoidable vulnerabilities that accompany human life. Martha Nussbaum reframes the question: "How much should a rational plan of life allow for elements such as friendship, love, political activity, attachments to property or possessions, all of which, being themselves vulnerable, makes the person who stakes his or her good to them similarly open to chance?" How shall a person pursue the freedom of a good life while remaining a "hostage to fortune"?

Paul Ricoeur defines human flourishing as "the good life, lived with and for others, in just institutions." Restated, this definition reminds us that our life will not thrive if we remain alone, or if we live only for ourselves, or if we live without the security of institutions whose laws provide safe harbor for us all.

Ricoeur clarifies the dilemma of human flourishing by distinguishing two dynamics in moral life: an *ethics of aspiration* and a *morality of obligation*. In his vision morality defines the realm of law and duty, the social norms that constrain and protect us. Ethics, on the other hand, is concerned with personal conscience and the desires of the heart. While morality focuses on the universal and the obligatory, ethics focuses on the particular and the desirable. For Ricoeur, then, conscience is more than the mere arbiter of obligation. Running beneath the social framework of laws and norms, conscience provides for each person the most immediate intuition of the good life. While attending to the rules of social morality, a person must also "return to the initial intuition of ethics," that is, to the vision of one's own flourishing life, with and for others in just institutions.

Ricoeur's insight leads to an understanding of human flourishing as *satisfying engagement, with valued others, in worthwhile activity*. Put negatively, genuine happiness will be difficult to achieve if we live and work only by ourselves, if we are engaged principally with people we neither value nor trust, or if the activities and projects that occupy our effort do not seem worthwhile.

What does Christian discipleship have to do with human flourishing? What does happiness have to do with commitment to follow Jesus Christ? In *A Secular Age* Taylor examines the relationship between secular humanism, with its concerns for human flourishing, and a Christian perspective on a full life. He seeks to reinforce a Christian humanism whose ideals stretch beyond the immediate here and now. In the Christian vision human "flourishing is good, nevertheless seeking it is not our highest goal." The Christian story, with its narratives of losing and gaining life, honors "the insight that we can find in suffering and death not merely negation, the undoing of fullness and life, but also a place to affirm something that matters beyond life." Acts of generosity (care for strangers in need) and acts of self-sacrifice (for one's children or for one's nation) serve as examples of the human impulse to transcend the narrow boundaries of individual flourishing.

Christian humanism celebrates both the values that are worth living for and ideals that may be worth dying for. The sacrifice of one's own resources—even one's life—for others is difficult to justify or explain in secular terms. For Taylor, happiness is too thin an ideal to stake one's life on. A full and meaningful life will almost certainly be a blend of failure and achievement, of sacrifice as well as delight.

For many religious people the human capacity for transcendence (the relentless desire for *something else* and *something more*) resonates with Taylor's conviction that "the point of things isn't exhausted by life." With joy as emotional response to the good news and consolation as a mood that buoys our spirit in a bewildering, wounded world, we seek the happiness we were born for, even in the midst of loss and suffering. And we give thanks for the human flourishing that, from time to time, blesses this journey.

7

Transformations of Love

It was you who formed my inmost parts;
You knit me together in my mother's womb.
I praise you for I am fearfully and wonderfully
made.

—PSALM 139

Love is not a single emotion but an extended family of feelings. Love encompasses both early romance and parental devotion; the life-long affection that develops between spouses as well as camaraderie among friends; a caregiver's commitment to the person in need and the affection we feel for those who have cared for us. Many of us would include religious devotion and heartfelt compassion among our own significant experiences of love. These relationships differ in emotional tone and in the behavior that follows. Each can be a profound expression of love, but they are not the same. The shape of our loving depends on the particular relationship involved.

Psychologists are eager to understand how we develop our capacity to love well. Many agree that our initial experiences of *attachment* are the foundation for all the works of love that follow. Attachment theory traces the emotional roots of love to the dynamics that unfold in early parent-child interaction. These early patterns set out a framework of how—as adults—we respond to critical dimensions of our relational world: closeness and separation, strength and vulnerability, pleasure and injury, affirmation and antagonism.

Dynamics of Early Attachment

A mother stands over the crib, gently stroking her infant as she speaks comforting words. The baby's eyes widen as he, in turn, utters indistinct sounds—babbles and coos that delight the attentive parent. The mother laughs, and the baby's face lights up as his limbs move with excitement. Later in the day, when the baby cries, his father lifts him in a warm embrace, looking into his eyes as he rocks the child in his arms. Both parents become eager participants in this charming exchange. In all these physical embraces—of sight and sound and touch—neural paths are laid down in the brains of both parents and the child. These neural patterns record and reinforce effective patterns of care-seeking and caregiving behavior.

Care-seeking is the healthy human start on the developmental journey that will make us competent lovers. The healthy baby begins life as a recruiter; the helpless infant has to be successful in drawing the attention of nearby adults and soliciting their effective care. The evolutionary purpose of such recruiting is clear. As Siegel writes, "Proximity seeking allows an infant to be protected from harm, starvation, unfavorable temperature changes, disasters, attacks from others, and separation from the group." When care-seeking is successful, the child learns that security comes in closeness. When we draw near to other people, our needs will be acknowledged and very often met. Even toddlers, who can move about on their own, still find safety in a quick return to their caregiver—running back to mother or father—holding a parent's hand in novel or dangerous situations.

In the everyday exchanges of holding, feeding and consoling their infants, attentive parents create an abiding mood of comfort and safety—a reservoir of trust on which the child's later experiments in friendship and love will depend. From these repeated exchanges the child learns that dependence is not shameful and that vulnerability need not be denied or disguised. With this secure base the child is better equipped to make his or her way into the exciting turmoil of adult life.

Care-seeking behavior by the infant evokes an adult response. Parents and other caregivers try to read the baby's arousal accurately and move to offer aid and solace. The attentiveness involved in recognizing and responding to the infant's needs develops resources in the adult caregiver, as well as assuring protective presence for the child. This interplay lays the foundation for mutual empathy, as child and caregiver become alert and responsive to each other's feelings and moods.

Attachment theory suggests that emotional experiences in infancy release the resources that humans need to care for other people and to respond to their love in return. These resources are crucial in adult life, supporting our efforts to establish and maintain the life-giving commitments of love. Even as adults, especially during times of stress, we continue to depend on the bonds of attachment. In our faithful companions—family and close friends, mentors and trustworthy colleagues—we find sources of comfort and strength.

But not all of us have been blessed with such attentive and affectionate caregivers. With parents who are absent or unreliable in their responses—physically or emotionally—children are likely to grow up cautious in relationships, finding it difficult to trust others and turning away from commitments that might open them to dependence and vulnerability.

Readying the Brain for Relationship

Daniel Siegel identifies attachment behavior as an inborn capacity of the human species: "Seeking proximity to a caregiver and attaining face-to-face communication with eye contact is hardwired into the brain from birth. It is not learned." Though this early recruiting behavior is hard-wired, the infant's underdeveloped brain requires continuing formation. "Human infants have profoundly underdeveloped brains. Maintaining proximity to their caregivers is essential, both for survival and for allowing their brains to use the mature states of the attachment figure to help them organize their own mental functioning."

Emotional Resonance

In early experiences of attachment a child is forming the capacity to develop emotional relationships. To understand the significance of this capacity, we need to appreciate the process through which the brain undergoes structural change from experience. Siegel explains, "The neural networks around the heart and throughout the body are intimately interwoven with the resonance circuits in the brain." These networks are the foundation of *limbic memory,* the settled brain patterns that influence how we will respond to other people. Siegel describes this resource as *resonance,* that is, an emotional attunement to another's emotional states that is the bedrock of sustained adult intimacy. Emotional resonance lays the foundation for mutual empathy, as child and caregiver become alert and responsive to each other's feelings and moods.

Emotional Recognition

As children we are introduced to our own feelings secondhand. Only through emotional resonance with another person can we begin to appreciate our own inner world. Parents' responses to the small child—through touch, words, actions—demonstrate how to respond to emotional stimulation; especially significant are the emotions and behaviors that the child sees displayed in response to stress. Here the well-cared-for child learns that closeness carries both protection and pleasure. These first few years of successful resonance prepare our emotional brain for a lifetime's use.

Emotional Regulation

When we have experienced attentive caregiving in childhood, Siegel notes, "this helps us to develop the internal strength of self-regulation, to become focused, thoughtful, and resourceful." Having benefited from effective early attachment, we enter adult life with a capacity for intimate relationships. Confident that our own vulnerability is healthy and that dependence on others is not demeaning, we are more ready to risk the closeness that accompanies mature intimacy.

Emotional Revision

Those with whom we establish close emotional relationships throughout life can both reinforce earlier emotional patterns and—when necessary—help new and more adaptable patterns to emerge. The plasticity of the human brain holds out this promise. In an adult relationship with a person who shows us attentive care and is comfortable with our feeling world, we can become more accurately in touch with our own feelings. Seigel notes: "The presence of a caring, trusted other person, one who is attuned to our internal world, is often the initial key." When we are supported by sensitive human presence—in friendship, in psychological counseling, in spiritual direction—the neural connections required for mature attachment will begin to emerge. Here the limbic brain's adaptive capacity can be recruited for therapeutic healing.

The Benefits of Attachment

The lessons of successful attachment are crucial. Early attachment promotes self-awareness. In relationship with attentive adults the child comes to appreciate that the self has many dimension. Responses from early caregivers give us information about our strengths and limitations. In their eyes we see reflected both the *good me* and the *bad me,* and these evaluations become the basis of our sense of ourselves. The movement into our own adulthood will demand that we reexamine these early evaluations as we come to appreciate the range of arousals and responses that are part of what it means to be *me*.

Through attachment we learn that close relationships nurture our growth and development. Those we come to depend on will support us emotionally, even as they refuse to take advantage of our weakness. Both strengths and limits will be known here and honored here, but the goal is that we may be stronger. The gift of close relationships is the strengthening of our best self.

Early attachment brings additional benefits. The still-vulnerable child learns that it is safe to explore the environment, because others are nearby to cover the risks. This early experience of attentive companionship supports freedom and spontaneity. It is safe for us to expand the range of our life experiences, to attempt something new. We can trust ourselves in novel situations because we have learned that we are not alone or unprotected.

These gifts of successful attachment carry over into adult life. We've learned the earlier lesson that it is good to be close to other people. Closeness brings protection, closeness carries delight, closeness strengthens self-esteem. These blessings are not realized in every relationship, so learning the perils of closeness is equally important. But effective attachment helps us approach other people with positive expectations.

Through secure attachment we have learned that risk and trust are related. We grow more comfortable in acknowledging even our vulnerability, assured that those close to us will not take unfair advantage of our needs. And as we know, without vulnerability, intimacy cannot and does not exist.

Attachment behavior opens us to those who respond to *me* in particular. The responses most significant to us come not from *just anybody* but from emotionally relevant sources. And what we are looking for in closeness and care is not just practical resources for problem solving, but the attentive presence of another person.

These resources of secure attachment are reinforced in mutual relationships. Mutual love attunes us to each other *in particular*. We hold each other in sensitive loving care. Each of us recognizes "I am *special* here," even if we are not the exclusive focus of the each other's concern. In mutual love we are attentive to each other, and we are mindful of the relationship itself. Appreciating that sometimes our relationship will need tending, we both take responsibility for keeping the lines of communication clear. And we share responsibility for repairing our relationship when ordinary tensions or extraordinary events in life lead us to question our commitment to each other.

Spiritual Attachment: We Belong to a Jealous God

"Jealousy is the perception that your ability to come to favorable terms with another person is threatened each time the desired individual becomes entangled with other people." Roberto Unger continues: "If jealousy had its way, the desired person would be isolated as much and for as long as possible from other people." His definition reminds us that most often jealousy registers as a moral fault. Yet the biblical accounts in Exodus and Deuteronomy, testifying to Yahweh's fierce attachment to his people, proclaim that ours is a jealous God (Ex 20:5; 34:14; Dt 6:14).

Early in Israel's religious memory Yahweh had offered this assurance: "I shall be your God and you shall be my people." Yet the chosen people needed constant reminders of the ties that bound them to their God. Other deities appeared in their land, eliciting allegiance that threatened the covenant. With vigilant concern Yahweh demanded that Israel reject such disloyalty and honor its attachment to the one true God. God's fierce attention focused on protecting this bond of mutual love.

In the biblical languages of Hebrew and Greek (and in English, for that matter), the term *jealous* is closely related to *zealous*. The Oxford English Dictionary retains some of this connection: *jealousy* is defined as "zeal with vehemence of feeling." Both terms point to a powerful emotional attachment that is ready to fend off all rivals. Yahweh's jealous/zealous attachment to the nation of Israel was remembered in the gospel story of Jesus violently overturning the merchants' tables set up in front of the temple. Reflecting on this angry outburst Jesus' disciples recalled the biblical judgment: "Zeal for your house will consume me" (Jn 2:17). Writing to the Christians in Corinth, Paul describes the "holy jealousy" that registers his concern for this community (2 Cor 11:2); he thanks the members here for their affectionate "zeal for me," which leaves him consoled and comforted (2 Cor 7:12). In these biblical passages *jealous* and *zealous* are rendered by the same Greek word.

Elsewhere in the New Testament (see Acts 7:9; 1 Cor 3:3; Jas 2:17), *jealousy* comes closer to the contemporary negative sense. But to appreciate the fierce attachment of God's universal love, it is important even now to acknowledge both meanings. *Jealous* names the heightened emotion of this enduring attachment; *zealous* identifies readiness to do whatever is necessary to strengthen and secure this life-giving relationship.

The Emotion of *Amae*: Attachment, Japanese Style

Cultures customize emotions, shaping them through language and nuance. The Japanese culture recognizes a particular expression of mature attachment identified as *amae*. Appreciating this culturally distinct emotion enhances our understanding of the power of attachment at both the psychological and religious levels.

In the Japanese culture the emotion of *amae* describes a sense of attachment and healthy dependence that begins in infancy and continues as an integral strength of adult maturity. As Takeo Doi explains, *amae* is the feeling of affection and secure belonging that originates in the parent-child bond. Japanese dictionaries list the qualities associated with this term: "to avail oneself of another's kindness . . . to be spoiled."

Doi expands the nuances of this particularly Japanese emotion. In *amae* a person expects to be indulged, to be permitted to be playful or silly or spontaneous. In a more problematic expression, *amae* is "to presume too much," to be too optimistic. Thus a frequently indulged child may ask too much of other people's indulgence or naively expect the world to be immediately responsive to his or her personal needs or demands. But as a healthy sense of dependence, *amae* functions as both an emotion and a strategy of belonging. This special affective bond lies at the root of the powerful Japanese sense of loyalty to family, corporation and nation.

Doi offers a telling example of his encounter with Western self-reliance during an early visit in the United States. At the first cocktail party he attended in this country the hostess approached him with a warm welcome. She then pointed to the nearby table, abundantly laid out with food and drink, and encouraged him to "help yourself." To his Japanese sensitivity this suggestion seemed most peculiar; the implication was that no one else was going to help him! In the Japanese culture hospitality demands that a guest be indulged, be able to presume on the host's initial welcome and continuing attention. Without this experience of *amae*, the guest feels neglected, set adrift in a sea of independent party goers.

The cultural commitment in the United States to self-reliance sometimes leaves us ambivalent about emotional closeness. In our commitment to individualism, Americans tend to see adult dependence as weakness and immaturity. Such passive reliance on others is seen as a characteristic of childhood, to be set aside as one matures. The emotion of *amae*, with its distinct interpretation of adult relationships, may invite Westerners to reflect on the limits of our own ideals of autonomy.

Attachment—Indulged by Friends and by a Loving God

The indulgence that lies at the core of *amae* is, in fact, not unknown to us. Spouses or friends sit quietly in the same room, each busy with private details that demand personal concentration. Comfortable with each other's attention focused elsewhere, they remain very much in each other's presence. This scene reveals the treasured interdependence of adult intimacy. It may also capture the religious believer's relationship with God. Faith allows us to bask in the presence of a loving Creator and steadfast Provider. Grace then is the fundamental energy on which we presume and rely.

Biblical accounts of *finding favor* may assist us, as Western Christians, to appreciate this highly nuanced emotion of *amae*. Receiving and granting favor lies at the heart of the human exchanges through which we flourish. And this is true in our relationship with a loving God. Scripture's earliest word for *grace* meant *favor*, the indulgent care and healing support with which God *favors* us. Thus we may speak of the indulgent attachment of *amae* as a grace. This comes to us as gift; without it we fail to flourish. And because this emotion is first stirred in us by our parents, we remember Jesus calling God *abba*, father. Abba suggests not an all-powerful and stern judge but a loving, indulgent daddy, one on whom we forever depend. For Christians, *abba* may open the door to *amae*.

Attachment and the Transformations of Love

Therefore, a man will leave his father and his mother, and cling to his wife and they will become one flesh.

—GENESIS 2:24

Exiting childhood with a sense of a secure attachment—with abiding memories of being reliably held with affection and protection—prepares us for the enlivening encounters of adult relationships. Blessed by experiences of intimacy shared and vulnerability respected, we respond with confidence to the thrill of romance. We embrace the challenges of committed love, strengthened by resources of fidelity and devotion. These engagements regularly form us in the rhythm of attachment and detachment.

Roberto Unger says it well: "We present to one another both an unlimited need and an unlimited danger." There is only one way through the impasse. Unger continues, "To satisfy our longing for acceptance and recognition, to be intimately assured that we have a place in the world, we must open ourselves to personal attachments and communal engagements whose terms we cannot predefine and whose course we cannot control."

For some of us, earlier religious formation included warnings about "becoming attached to the things of this world," warnings that have left us suspicious of the embraces of adult life. Being attached to a "jealous God" may require, we have been cautioned, a thorough detachment from everything else. This caution has led some devout Christians to the conclusion that other people in our life should be held at a distance lest they become objects of "inordinate attachment."

Fortunately, in contemporary discussions of Christian spirituality attachment is reemerging as a necessary and healthy dynamic. Faith itself, we realize, is an experience of religious attachment; we cling to the Mystery from which we have emerged and to which we are returning. The virtues of hope and fidelity are attachments without which faith will not thrive. To be sure, "inordinate attachments" continue to abound. These include not only the addictive behaviors that endanger health and happiness, but also distracting concerns for wealth and reputation that leave us "so loving our life that we lose it." But healing attachments also abound, strong bonds of fidelity with those whom we hold in our love and care; dedication to ideals that motivate our career and prompt our participation in the common good. Through these committed forms of devotion we grow more rooted in our vocational call and even more secure in attachment to God.

The Ingredients of Romance

Love thrives in attachments. The attachments of romance, commitment, fidelity and devotion unfold over a lifetime. Perhaps the most pervasive model of love in U.S. culture is romance. What goes on in romantic love? Three elements are central. The first is *powerful attraction*. Romance draws us together physically and emotionally. When we are apart, we long for the other's presence; when we are near, we feel exhilarated. The allure can be overwhelming. We feel swept away. The forces at play are "bigger than both of us"; they seem to be outside—even beyond—our conscious choice. We speak of the magnetism we feel, the chemistry between us. These images capture the sense that we are caught up in something beyond our control. In this excitement the sexual component is strong. Lovers may choose to reserve genital expression until after the formal commitment of marriage, but sexual energy is high.

Second, romance celebrates a sense of *fitness*. In romantic love a strong (even if not always accurate) awareness of congruence and compatibility emerges. We are convinced that we are perfectly suited for each other, that "we fit together well." We like the same things; we have the same hopes for our love; we agree on what is important in life; we never argue. Romance, then, links us in values and vision as well as in affection and attraction.

Third, romance holds out the *promise of the future*. If our shared present holds such delight, surely a common future holds even more. This sense of promise fuels the decision to take on the broader commitments of married life and parenting. Romance leads us into marriage with powerful hopes of what our future will hold. Together, we want to shape a life that guarantees the love we know now and realizes our shared vision of an even richer future.

As many of us know from personal experience, romance does not always keep these promises. The potential of romance is not necessarily fulfilled in the ongoing experience of our relationship. This doesn't necessarily mean that romance always deceives, or that it carries no truth. But the maturing of love may well involve some purification of the expectations that come to us in romance.

From Romance to Chosen Commitment

Mature love is expressed in a cognitive, behavioral and emotional stance toward another. Gradually this beloved's well-being becomes as important to us as is our own. We are willing to sacrifice our own comfort, even our own safety, on this person's behalf. In love we stand ready to devote our time, our resources, and our ingenuity to supporting the one we love. Our relationship matures as the arousals of early attraction and romance expand to include a love that is a chosen and cultivated commitment.

This expansion can widen to include the breadth of a love that is named *agape* or *caritas*. The expression of unconditional love is central in the ethical systems of most of the world's great religion traditions. Love draws energy from its arousals—of compassion, of altruistic concern. But love as *caritas* or *agape* is more than an emotional arousal. Love fuels unselfish actions that move us beyond ourselves. Perhaps it is more accurate to say that love matures as it draws on the energy of romance to nurture a wider range of responsiveness and responsibility.

Psychologists today discuss love as a moral disposition, as a character trait and as an enduring personal capacity. This capacity is rooted in the emotional resource of intimacy. Intimacy names the ability to commit ourselves to a particular person in a relationship that lasts over time. Intimacy moves us beyond idealized expectations to embrace real persons in their particular uniqueness (and peculiarity!). Intimacy strengthens the intellectual and emotional resources that enable us to pledge our future, based only on what we know in the present. From one perspective this might seem a foolish endeavor; the future is unknown. How can we pledge ourselves to be constant when so much of the future remains hidden? Who will you be, who will I be, what practical circumstances will shape our life together? Yet without this capacity to pledge our future, we will remain alone—we will not thrive.

From Commitment to Fidelity

Romance matures in committed love and bears fruit in fidelity. Erik Erikson defines fidelity as the ability to sustain mutual loyalties that have been freely pledged in the face of inevitable contradictions and conflicts that arise in any ongoing relationship.

Fidelity recognizes that our commitments in love are *freely* pledged, that we can take them back. But fidelity sustains our loyalty, even in the face of the inevitable difficulties that arise between us or are provoked by larger circumstances of our lives. Fidelity makes mature love possible. The virtue of fidelity does not prevent problems from arising, but fidelity gives us the resilient strength to honor our commitments, even as we recognize the contradictions that confront us now or overshadow us from the past. James Cotter celebrates this face of love in *Homosexual and Holy*, when he writes of "those finer vibrations of pleasure that come from the complete trust that two people have in each other when they are faithful over a long period of time."

From Fidelity to Devotion

The transformations of love—from the rush of romance to the affection of intimacy to the strength of fidelity—come together in mutual devotion. Devotion proclaims that someone else's well-being is as important to us as our own. And we, too, are held in that treasured embrace; our well-being is significant to those who truly love us.

Devotion is evident in a love that is *well aged*. Accustomed over decades to each other's ways—both the endearing and the maddening—we know each other well. Now, grateful and still in love, we enjoy growing old together. The youthful passion of romance has been transmuted into a mellow affection.

Devotion often shows its extraordinary strength in the face of diminishment and death. In *Elegy for Iris* John Bayley writes of the final years with his wife, the philosopher and novelist Iris Murdoch. He traces their life together as she succumbs to Alzheimer's disease. Married for more than forty years, these two British academics had led eccentric lives. Childless, their two careers and diverse interests often meant long periods of time spent apart. The onset of Iris's illness forced dramatic changes in this arrangement. "After more than forty years of taking marriage for granted, marriage had decided it is tired of this and is taking a hand in the game. Purposefully, persistently, involuntarily, our marriage is now getting somewhere."

As her illness progressed, John could not face placing Iris into a residential care facility. Speaking of their own situation he writes: "She grows agitated when he is away, and he loses his purpose when he is alone." In a poignant witness to devotion, he adds, "I don't know what to do with myself when she's not there." Two thousand years earlier the Roman author Plutarch wrote his own testimony to devoted love: "The love of a virtuous woman suffers no autumn but flourishes even with gray hair and wrinkles." Another image of devotion: *eros* with wrinkles.

8

Virtues of Pride and Humility

I often boast about you; I have great pride in you! I am filled with consolation and am over-joyed even in my affliction.

—2 Corinthians 7:4

Pride names that expansive feeling in our chest as we watch our child perform well in a school drama or sports event. This positive emotion stirs as we applaud the success of a good friend's risky venture. An older couple look back over their life together with a sense of satisfaction mingled with the feeling of pride. And in our life of faith we recognize that, despite our flaws and failings, we are crafted in the image of God. This, too, is something to be proud of.

Willard Gaylin suggests that pride is one of our "vital signs . . . basic to the survival apparatus of a thinking and social animal." The emotion of pride delights in the good and the beautiful, in achievements both small and large. Pride renders a judgment of worth and excellence. As a moral emotion pride is anchored in gratitude and abides in self-respect. Pride is part of the chorus that celebrates creation's goodness.

Parental pride is the bedrock of this emotion. Gaylin writes: "We are proud of them [our children] beyond their necessary warrant of pride. Children, being our ultimate products, our best hope for immortality, need do little but exist to produce the feeling of pride." But the Christian Gospels had long ago alerted us to this parental exaltation. At the baptism of Jesus a voice is heard: "This is my beloved son of whom I am most proud" (Lk 3:22). St. Paul writes to the Christian community in Corinth: "I often boast about you; I have great pride in you! I am filled with consolation and am overjoyed even in my afflictions" (2 Cor 7:4).

77

Healthy pride is an achievement in the growing child. In his research on human development Erik Erikson examined the emergence of this essential strength. Between eighteen months and three years of age children learn to move about on their own. And gradually they move away from total dependence on their parents' care and control. Parents now must contend with this emergence of personal willfulness. This period, appropriately identified as "the terrible twos," is critical in the child's development of autonomy and agency. Success in navigating this psychological task is registered in self-determination: the child takes pleasure in newfound self-control (toilet training) and self-assertion (refusing to eat the food offered). Augustine, describing his own childhood, recalled that "by various cries and sounds and movements of my limbs I tried to express my inner feelings and get my will obeyed." This burgeoning sense of self-confidence—which Erikson identifies as the virtue of pride—becomes an essential resource throughout adult life.

This developmental achievement establishes an initial balance between personal freedom and our enduring dependence on other people. Here, too, we confront the challenge of self-acceptance: we are lovely (and so there is reason to be proud), and also limited (and so there is reason to be cautious). These dynamics of strength and weakness, experienced again and again over a lifetime, shape the movements of healthy pride and appropriate humility. Failing to reach a sense of self as both capable and vulnerable, we risk living off balance, constantly scanning other people's responses to gauge our own worth. This approach to life is governed not by humility but by shame.

The positive emotion of pride, again in Gaylin's words, "involves a sense of well-being; a general awareness of one's self; of being worthy, of being decent. In this sense it is synonymous with self-respect." As a moral emotion pride broadens and builds our inner resourcefulness. Feelings of pride enhance a sense of self-worth and encourage future behaviors that strengthen this worthiness. "I view pride as a virtue and its absence as the deficiency of our time. Self-respect and self-value are essential components of the capacity for pleasure and performance which . . . is so essential to adult maturity," Gaylin concludes.

Pride as Vice—Healthy Pride's Evil Twin

In ordinary usage the word *pride* carries two conflicting meanings. As a moral emotion pride signals a self-respect that is "one of our vital signs." But the same word is used to identify a sense of self-worth gone wrong. Aberrant expressions of pride abound in our culture: the vanity cultivated by the cosmetic and fashion industries; the arrogance of those—politicians, professors, pastors—who insist they know what is best for the rest of us; the narcissism of those for whom every conversation must ultimately focus on themselves. Perhaps another example emerges from the pervasive sense of entitlement in American society. Many of us act out of the conviction that, as Americans, we deserve all the advantages we have received . . . and more. We deserve "the very best" and resent having to pay higher taxes to support these benefits. This unblushing sense of entitlement may be our most pernicious cultural expression of pride as a vice.

Pride in the Bible

Examples of both healthy and sinful pride are found in scripture. In the Hebrew bible the Israelites exhibited justifiable pride in their position as God's chosen people. In the Book of Leviticus we read of God's promise to maintain the covenant, to dwell among them and to make them walk heads held high.

The Book of Proverbs cautions repeatedly against sins of pride and arrogance. "Pride and arrogance . . . I hate" (8:13). "When pride comes, then comes disgrace; but wisdom is for the humble; the integrity of the upright guides them" (11:2–3). "Pride goes before destruction; and a haughty spirit before the fall" (16:18).

In the New Testament we find Paul's heartfelt pride in the Christian community in Corinth. "I often boast about you; I have great pride in you! I am filled with consolation and overjoyed even in my afflictions" (2 Cor 7:4). And in Jesus' baptism in the Jordan River, God's great delight shines out: "This is my beloved son of whom I am most proud" (Lk 3:22).

Elsewhere in the New Testament, Jesus reacts harshly to the arrogance of the self-righteous and self-important: "You hypocrite! First take the log out of your own eye, then you will see clearly to take the speck out of your neighbor's eye" (Mt 7:5). Luke's Gospel assures us that "God will scatter the proud" (1:51). New Testament expressions for sinful pride are often registered as bodily emotions. So we read of the proud being "puffed up" (1 Tm 3:6; 6:4); in English we make a similar reference to the self-absorbed person as "full of himself." The First Letter of John cautions against the "swagger" that accompanies a love of riches (1 Jn 2:16). In Jerome's Latin text of the New Testament these "embodied" verbs are translated by the abstract term *superbia* (thinking oneself superb). Here pride is transformed from physical behavior to mental attitude.

Pride in the Early Church

The first generations of Christians, struggling to find their way amid the distractions and temptations of the Roman Empire, were of two minds. On the one hand, they knew themselves to be created in the image of God and were now God's chosen people— clearly attributes to generate pride. Bishop Irenaeus in the second century proclaimed that "the glory of God is man fully alive." Our humanity, despite its multiple limitations, reflects the very glory of God. This, too, is a cause for rejoicing.

But, on the other hand, during these same early centuries a more pessimistic attitude toward humanity was also at play. Recognizing that human nature is chronically injured by sin and destined for death, thoughtful writers raised caution. Augustine, as we have seen, argued that humans have been so corrupted by sin that they are incapable of goodness. Whatever good that might break the surface of their sinfulness can only be due to God's grace. Sinful humanity, with its lustful temptations and self-deception, has no basis for self-congratulations. In fact, for Augustine every personal sin was itself an exercise in pride, part of humankind's perverted sense of its self-justification. In truth, we have nothing of which we can be proud. Sin involves our stepping out of this lowly status and assuming a role beyond our rightful place. In the same century, as monastic piety developed the list of seven deadly sins, human pride held pride of place.

Pride in Contemporary Life

Pride reflects the value we ascribe to our talents and achievements. Healthy pride rejoices in generous effort and genuine achievement. Unhealthy pride, the Oxford English Dictionary warns, is rooted in an "inordinate self-esteem." Here our self-evaluation is distorted. Under the illusion of self-sufficiency, we assume sole responsibility for our success. American culture reinforces this fiction in its ideal of the self-made man, who pulls himself up "by his own bootstraps." No solace is wasted on those who do not fit this self-sufficient mold. But the ideal of self-sufficiency—and its emotional marker, self-esteem—has its critics today, even in the United States.

Up to the mid twentieth century a spiritual perspective prevailed, perhaps especially among American Catholics, that favored maintaining a low opinion of oneself as safeguard against the sin of pride. Virtue demanded downplaying personal achievements and refusing compliments, on principle. At play was a larger cultural demand to "know one's place" in life. Protective of class distinctions, this attitude saw ambition as a challenge to social stability. To aspire for what was beyond one's "station in life" was unruly and prideful. In church life this attitude demanded that women—and lay people in general—"know their place."

The transformations of American society taking place in the 1960s challenged this approach to self-regard. Symbolic of the changing attitude was the Self-esteem movement. Designed to encourage self-confidence in children, this movement quickly morphed into what many critics saw as uncritical extolling of children's abilities. From this unbalanced enthusiasm arose what has been described as a culture of narcissism or self-absorption.

Pride and Self-Sufficiency

Unhealthy pride thrives on the illusion of self-sufficiency. Our life goes wrong when we are unmindful that all our strengths—beginning with life itself—come as gift. Our view becomes distorted when we lose sight of the relationships that support, foster and forgive us on our journey. In recent decades American Christians have struggled to craft a healthy celebration of their talents linked with a gratefulness for these strengths as gifts.

Spirituality is always about overcoming forgetfulness. Once we become privileged by fortune with financial success, we are tempted to judge that the less fortunate have simply failed to apply themselves. Immigrants (this generation of newcomers, not our own immigrant forebears) are seen as inferior and undeserving. We stand apart and above the poor, the unfortunate, the foreigner. So the sin of pride takes root.

Roberto Unger describes the sin of pride not as rising up beyond one's proper status, but as an unhealthy effort to disengage. Eager to detach from dependence on others, struggling to free ourselves from the entanglements of social life, we are drawn in the direction of pride. In Unger's words: "You stand aloof from others; you do not subject yourself to the risk of the equivocal, the ridiculous, the humiliating." But the irony of this aspiration for excellence is that it renders a person hostage to the evaluation of others. Unger writes, "Vanity is the surrender of self-esteem to the opinions of other people."

Paul's Dilemma—Boasting of His Weakness

Leaders frequently feel the need to remind us of all they have done for us. But while pursuing this course—pointing to the successes achieved and the suffering endured for the sake of the group—the leader is likely to feel foolish, recognizing the futility of such appeals.

Paul, writing to the Christians in Corinth, surrendered to this need to boast. But even as he lists his many accomplishments, Paul acknowledges some awkwardness. Toward the end of his second letter to the members of this community he asks them "to bear with me in a little foolishness" as he boasts about what he has endured to bring the gospel message to them. There follows a long list of the adversities he has suffered—imprisonment, flogging, shipwreck, many sleepless nights while hungry and thirsty.

Then, paradoxically, Paul shifts the focus of his account. He now boasts of his personal weakness, rejoicing that God has seen fit to work through him in spite of his limitations. Paul has learned that his own infirmity (his "thorn in the flesh") is a reason to boast because God's "power is made perfect in weakness" (2 Cor 12:9).

Pride here is not in Paul himself but in God's saving presence and activity. This theme is central in Paul's instructions to the early faith communities. In his First Letter to the Corinthians he writes, "Let the one who boasts, boast in the Lord" (1:31). And in a letter to the Galatians we read, "May I never boast of anything except the cross of our Lord Jesus Christ" (6:14). To the Romans he writes, "We boast in our hope of sharing the glory of God" (5:2).

The word that Paul uses here (the Latin word is *gloriare*) may be translated "boasting," but it may also be rendered as "to glory in" or "to exalt in." *Boasting* we associate with prideful behavior: bragging about one's exploits or accomplishments. *To glory in* carries different connotations. We glory in our children's successes, and we experience this same emotion with our national flag, "Old Glory." The term *glory* rings throughout scripture as well as in contemporary usage. The Hebrew word *kabod* suggests God's mysterious power and majesty: "Glory be to God." Here *glory* means "to praise." More curious is the mysterious encounter of Moses and Yahweh on Mount Sinai. Moses, eager to draw closer to his fascinating God, pleads "show me your glory" (Ex 33:18). This presence, which biblical scholar Leon-Dufour translates as "flashing radiance," is a blinding epiphany of God. The New Testament testifies that this divine glory shines forth in the face of Christ (2 Cor 4:6). Living in this powerful presence, Christians praise the glorious God. And communities of faith eagerly embrace those leaders who, following Paul, glory in the grace of Christ that shines through their efforts of faithful service.

Humility: Partner of Healthy Pride

Avis Clendenen writes, "Humility is the ancient ever-new virtue that keeps us rooted in our earthiness and able to savor our human limits as gifts." For those with a healthy sense of pride—able to delight in the successes of others even as they are mindful of their own competence—humility means something close to integrity, comfort with oneself as both lovely and limited.

Writing about "the lost art of humility," Clendenen offers a concrete example of this blend of modesty with grateful pride. Following many years of leadership in higher education, a Catholic sister chose to spend her senior years ministering to the poor in Central America. After a decade of such service, and now in her eighties, she returned for one last visit to the village where she had begun this "new" ministry. Entering one of these homes she noticed several items pasted on the wall, as though in a shrine. The first, as expected, was a picture of Our Lady of Guadalupe. Next to it was a simply drawn portrait of Bishop Oscar Romero, who had some few years prior been assassinated in retaliation for his prophetic work for social justice. And finally, she saw a photo of herself. Startled by this unexpected tribute, she reported her response: "It was a moment of abject humility, wonder, awe, and gratitude I will never forget." Humility—"I am not worthy to be part of this group!"—blended with gratitude (and not a little pride) to be in such excellent company.

Here humility has little to do with humiliation. Instead, the feeling is one of being grounded. The etymological root of humility is *humis,* meaning "soil" or "earth"—the ground we walk on and the earth to which we return. *Humility* and *humanity* share the same linguistic root. For a person with a healthy sense of pride, humility is an aspect of self-respect. Humor and honor are also likely companions. Humor at our frailty and occasional foolishness helps to keep us humble; honor takes pride in what God has granted us.

Humility and Great-Heartedness

A clue to the companionship of pride and humility comes to us in the *Magnificat,* Mary's prayerful response to the angel's announcement of her role in God's plan of salvation. In this extraordinary text she humbly acknowledges her own lowliness as she recognizes the significance of the role to which she is being called.

> "My soul magnifies the Lord and my spirit rejoices in God my Savior. God has looked with favor on the littleness of God's servant; surely from now on all generations will call me blessed for the Mighty One has done great things for me and holy is his Name." (Lk 1:47)

Magnify here means "to praise lavishly," "to make much of." Mary, embracing her own insignificance, honors God who "has done great things for me." In her prayer these mighty actions will in fact redound to God's glory. All future generations will call her blessed, by the mighty hand of God.

Thomas Aquinas described the paradoxical link between humility and "doing great things" in his distinction between the virtues of humility and magnanimity (great-heartedness). "Humility restrains the appetite from aiming at great things *against right reason*. Magnanimity urges the mind to great things *in accord with right reason*." The arousal, the positive emotion, of magnanimity instills in a person the ambition to accomplish great things. Lee Yearley comments on Aquinas's definition: "Magnanimity concerns those grand actions that rest in a justified trust of the self. It leads a person both to be free of insignificant anxieties and to aspire to and undertake great and honorable projects." Theologian Josef Pieper offers his description of great-heartedness: "The high-minded person bows neither to confusion of the soul, nor to any man, nor to fate—but only to God."

For Aquinas, "Magnanimity makes a person deem himself worthy of great things in consideration of the gifts he holds from God." A Christian vocation invites the balancing of a humble estimation of one's place in the world and a powerful striving to accomplish great things. For Augustine, great-heartedness would always lie under the threat of self-deception; ambition was likely to surface as one more lust for self-promotion. Convinced that the only good he managed was from God, Augustine (great-hearted though he was) could not relish and rejoice in his many gifts.

Anthony Kenny comments on Aquinas's linkage of humility and magnanimity: "Humility . . . ensures that one's ambitions are based on a just assessment of one's defects. Magnanimity . . . ensures that they are based on a just assessment of one's gifts." If great-heartedness names the impulse to achieve great things, the virtue of pride names the grateful satisfaction in accomplishing a few of these.

Aquinas further clarifies the relation of these two virtues. Humility is part of the cardinal virtue of temperance; it counsels one to temper and restrain their ambition. Magnanimity is part of the virtue of courage; it counsels one to greater initiative and boldness in attempting to achieve great things. It is curious that humility has received such emphasis in the Christian tradition to the neglect of its complement, great-heartedness. Paul concludes his list of the many gifts that the Spirit gives the community of faith with the encouragement, "Be zealous for the greater gifts" (1 Cor 12:21).

The Genesis of False Humility

In the medieval world of Aquinas, as for Augustine before him, pride was acknowledged as a particular challenge for those in positions of power—popes, princes, military leaders. These people, of whom much was expected, were cautioned to restrain their ambition so as to avoid the sin of pride. But then—as today—those of whom little achievement is expected seldom needed instruction in humility. Women, people of color, persons with developmental disabilities, those who are economically poor have long been counseled to be patient and self-effacing and to "know their place." Preaching the dangers of pride to a society's underprivileged is not a praiseworthy moral strategy but something closer to malpractice. Other virtues are called for: self-respect, courage, persistence, nerve.

For those burdened by society's prejudice the call to humility often has a political purpose. Here humility's demand is to lower oneself, to deny one's rightful claims, to "lose one's voice" in a retreat into silence. Gaylin suggests that this abusive social strategy, hiding behind a mask of humility, must be recognized for what it is: "a sin, for it leads to despair and encourages a tolerance for inequity and injustice."

False humility is often expressed in an unquestioning obedience to authority. Here we sense the links between humility and shame; the threat of being shamed by those who have power in our lives is meant to keep us humble. And a wounded sense of shame may well display itself in behaviors that parody true humility.

In religious settings false humility insists that we have nothing to be proud of. Here obedience trumps every other virtue; risk and courage find little place in the person determined "not to draw attention to myself." This attitude leaves little room for our contribution to the *great things* that God has envisioned for the world.

Pride and humility are not adversaries. These resources are companions by which we know ourselves to be both resourceful and vulnerable. There are many reasons to be humble: we are able to accomplish so little; our best plans are so often defeated. But equally we find many reasons to take pride both in our heritage as children of God and in our good works. There is so much for which we are grateful. And the practice of reverence becomes salient here. Susan Neiman writes, "Reverence is awareness of human limits, it is what creates humility." And Paul Woodruff concurs: "Hubris [pride] is best understood simply as the opposite of reverence, in action or attitude."

Thus the paradox of a Christian life: On Ash Wednesday we acknowledge that we come from dust and unto dust we shall return. At the same time we glory in all God has done for us. On our good days we even dare to aspire to the great things that God plans for us. Our soul magnifies the Lord, and our spirit rejoices in God our Savior.

9

Compassion
and Self-Care

*If you want to be happy, practice compassion.
If you want others to be happy, practice compassion.*

—THE DALAI LAMA

Compassion names a remarkable human capacity: our heartfelt response to another person's pain. As an emotion, compassion encompasses a range of feelings—sympathy, sadness, affection, concern. Our compassion sometimes includes anger aroused by the harm we see done to another person; we may even feel guilt over our own complicity. In compassion these feelings are often accompanied by an urgent desire to alleviate someone else's distress.

The great religious traditions of the world have honored compassion as humanity's defining characteristic. In the New Testament, Jesus offers compelling models: the good Samaritan generously responds to a stranger in need; a father offers eager welcome and forgiveness to his prodigal son. In the Buddhist tradition the bodhisattva refuses to enter immediately into the joy of nirvana, choosing instead—out of compassion—to remain in the world, working to free those still engulfed by ignorance and suffering. Early in Chinese culture the Confucian sage Mencius begins his classic exploration of the moral emotions with the conviction that "all people are unable to stand another's suffering." And ancient Romans understood this essential moral sensitivity as *humanitas*—the core virtue required of every human being. Across cultures and over millennia the human community has acknowledged that to lack compassion is to be less than human.

Compassion: A Body-Based Emotion

The Hebrew bible and contemporary neurosciences agree that the moral emotion of compassion is rooted deep in the body. Compassion received classic expression in the biblical story of the two women sleeping with their newborn infants (1 Kgs 3). One infant dies in the night. At dawn the two mothers struggle over who will keep the single surviving child. King Solomon, impatient with the wrangling, threatens to cut the child in half, giving part to each woman. The mother of the living child cries out in compassion, begging the king to give the baby—her own child—to the other woman. While this will bring great pain and suffering to her, at least her child's life will be spared.

In the Hebrew language the word translated "compassion" shares the same root with "womb." Scripture scholar Phyllis Trible catches this resonance with her translation of the biblical account of the true mother's response: "Her *rahmin (womb)* or compassion grew warm and tender, and yearned for her child." The woman's compassion was registered in this physical response at the thought of her child suffering. This womb-resonant word for compassion appears throughout the Hebrew scriptures, often describing God's heartfelt affection for humanity. Here, as Trible notes, "we see the movement from the wombs of women to the compassion of God."

In the New Testament the metaphor shifts but does not leave the body: here we find compassion translated by the Greek word meaning "gut-wrenching." Several centuries later, in Jerome's Latin translation, compassion would again shift locations. Now described as *misericordia*—a heart for those in misery—the emotion still remains deeply rooted in our bodies.

As humans we are wired for compassion. Psychologist Dacher Keltner insists that "we have been designed to care about things other than the gratification of desire and the maximizing of self-interest." Compassion, he explains, "is a biologically based emotion rooted deep in the mammalian brain . . . the need to care for the vulnerable." He concludes, "Compassion shifts the mind in ways that increase the likelihood of taking pleasure in the improved welfare of others."

Learning to Care

It is in the up-close world of family and friends that we learn our earliest lessons in compassion. Here we first become aware of other people's feelings. From this early awareness we can develop the resources of empathy, the emotional and intellectual ability to experience the world from another person's perspective.

Psychologist Daniel Siegel uses the term *resonance* to name the intuitive awareness we have for our own bodily self, a sensitivity that supports our empathic attentiveness to others. This resonance begins in the womb as the fetus develops in harmony with the mother's body. In the early months after birth the intense interactions between the infant and attentive caregivers establish bonds of trust, strengthening the child's capacity for physiological resonance. This resonance provides a biological foundation for the psychological resource of empathy.

Empathy gives us an uncanny ability to participate in another person's inner world. This vital resource, which makes psychological mutuality possible, lets us enter others' lives without diminishing their dignity or manipulating their emotions for our own purposes. Through mature empathy we can be both linked and distinct.

Psychologists offer valuable insight into the role of empathy as the foundation of compassionate response. Empathy evokes a range of feelings. Some of these arousals in us *mirror* the emotional state of the other person. This mirroring activity helps us appreciate that person's situation, making us more alert to what the person is feeling. And when empathy's appraisal is accurate, we are better able to determine our own response, that is, in this particular setting what might most support this particular person.

Empathy shapes our response as we act to promote others' well-being. This mature skill strengthens our *emotional intelligence*. People differ in their capacity to respond to emotionally significant stimuli and in their ability to use this information to guide their actions with and toward other people. We need these empathic resources to help us carry out the sophisticated information processing that allows us to take another person's perspective. For example, we must be able to set aside—at least for the moment—our own immediate concerns so that we may be attentive to someone else's experience. We must have some degree of comfort with our own emotions so that our empathic arousals do not frighten or distract us.

Empathy supports altruistic behavior, but empathy is not yet compassion. Empathy can generate feelings, reflecting a sense that something has turned out badly. But for the mature expression of compassion to emerge, empathy's instinctive responsiveness needs to be nurtured and refined. Marc Hauser has pioneered psychological research in moral development. He tracks the dynamics involved: "From purely emotional forms of empathy that are reflexive, the child grows into a form of empathy that takes into account what others know, believe, and desire." And, Hauser continues, "it is only in a more mature period of development that empathy couples with reflection and awareness." Learning to interpret the moral significance of a situation helps us to assess the appropriate responses that are available to us. Mature empathy includes this kind of judgment, equipping us to recognize reasons and consequences for action.

Empathy can be disturbing. A baby may cry in response to a nearby infant's tears; a toddler might display distress over unfair treatment of another child in nursery school. As we move beyond childhood into adolescence and adult life, most of us develop strategies to moderate empathy's native sensitivity—in effect, to shield ourselves from other people's pain. For those growing up in a dysfunctional family these distancing strategies may have been life-saving. Those of us in helping professions—nurses and others who serve in health-care settings, counselors, teachers, ministers—recognize that it is helpful to have some of these distancing strategies available.

Practicing compassion invites us to become aware of these often necessary protective shields. Compassion sometimes urges us to accept—even welcome—the distressing feelings that arise in our attentive involvement in other people's lives. Here our emotional distress can be part of the energy that motivates our caring response and gives it staying power.

But personal distress does not always provoke an empathic response. Personal distress is self-oriented; our own painful memories and emotions become primary. Psychologists suggest that mature empathy moves us beyond a preoccupation with our own distress. And research supports this distinction, finding that empathic concern for others is regularly associated with altruistic helping behavior; self-oriented personal distress in the face of other people's problems often interferes with effective helping behavior.

There are important alerts here for those of us in the helping professions—health care, counseling, ministry—and those of us committed to action for social justice. The discipline of empathic maturity is to become more sensitive in discerning the experience of others. A particular challenge is to resist letting our own emotional pain overpower our accurate response to those in our care.

The A-I-M of Compassion

Compassion, like other complex moral emotions, unfolds gradually. A physiological *arousal* alerts us to a scene inviting compassion. This stirring triggers an interior *interpretation*: we recognize that genuine need exists here. Sometimes a caution quickly follows: "There is nothing I can do." But compassion prompts another interpretation: "I should do something!" Here we are *moved* to action, as we reach out to help the person in distress. Arousal, interpretation and movement are the A-I-M of compassion.

Recent research has pinpointed the physiological arousal that marks the first stirring of compassion. Watching the evening news we observe the scene of heroic firefighters dashing into a burning building to rescue persons trapped inside; or we see medical volunteers attempting life-saving surgery in an overcrowded foreign refugee camp. As we watch these events unfold, we may experience a tightness or warmth in our chest, a catch in our throat or perhaps even a tear in our eye.

Neuropsychologists tell us this is the work of the vagus nerve: "the body's caring organ . . . especially involved in generating care-taking behavior." Centered in the chest, this neural network activates in moments of compassion. Once activated, the vagus nerve stimulates the release of oxytocin, a neurotransmitter associated with nurturing behavior and feelings of closeness and trust. These arousals fuel our actions of caring response. This elevated vagus nerve activity, Keltner notes, "orients the individual to a life of greater warmth and social connection."

Awakened to someone else's distress, we must determine how to proceed. To resist becoming involved, we sometimes tell ourselves there is no great need here or that someone else will respond. But often more generous instincts prevail, arousing us to act. This desire to help, to take action to alleviate the pain of another person, is at the core of the emotion of compassion.

Compassion *moves* us. Sometimes we are moved to tears. But compassion's wider focus also moves us to active response—to do something to resolve a distressing situation that affects real people. Sympathy may respond from a safe distance, pity sometimes looks down in condescension, but compassion comes in close—close enough to be moved, close enough for solidarity with those in need.

Practicing Compassion

Compassion, then, is a spontaneous feeling—and much more. This wholehearted response can be cultivated, maturing into a character strength that shapes our moral life. We can embrace compassion as a formative and transformative practice. *Practice* has become an important theme in contemporary ethics and moral theology. For some thoughtful observers, traditional understandings of virtue have become too abstract, somewhat removed from the practical realities of moral action and ethical behavior. Focusing on compassion as a moral practice shifts our attention to behaviors. Practices are actions that we perform intentionally. Our *intention* is, by our conscious embrace of these behaviors, to link our life with a larger vision or value tradition: the witness of Jesus, the moral heritage of the Bible, the political vision of the common good. Our *goal* in adopting these ways of acting is that we may be transformed, that our own life and behavior may resonate with and reflect these significant values.

As a formative and transformative practice, compassion disposes us to see people in certain ways, to act toward them in certain ways, and to embrace certain feelings. With the eyes of compassion we recognize that the one who suffers here is like *me*. We share a common humanity, which marks us as both vulnerable and worthy of respect. And we share a blessed identity—beloved of God and enlivened by God's Spirit. People who act with compassion do so generously and without coercion. But even so, compassion makes a claim on us by widening the circle of *our kind,* those who have a right to our resources.

Practicing compassion, we are moved to act in certain ways. We may *act for* the one who suffers by offering practical assistance that is immediately needed. Or we join with those in need, *acting together* to resolve the present problem or confront the underlying injustice. And in circumstances that seem to defeat our best efforts, when action fails to resolve the pain, compassion steadies us for solidarity. Compassion moves us to stay involved, to continue to *stand with* those who suffer. And genuine compassion *acts with mutuality and respect*, honoring the autonomy and dignity of those who suffer. Aware of others' distress, conscious of their genuine need, empathy helps us avoid actions that will make matters worse.

Compassion is at play in our close relationships too. As we draw close, we come in contact with the faults and limitations of those who are our intimates. We are often affected, sometimes even offended, by one another's weaknesses. Aware of our own wounds and wounding behavior we can offer those who offend us the grace of compassion. Instead of punishment we move toward reconciliation—for the sake of other person and for the good of our ongoing relationship.

The Virtue of Self Compassion

Biblical stories of exceptional compassion encourage Christians to develop this sensitivity toward others in need, especially the most vulnerable. Rarely has the virtue of compassion been recognized as a kindness we are meant to extend to ourselves. Instead, many Christians have learned that acknowledgment of their own sinfulness demands constant, critical surveillance. They have learned to apply unrealistic—and unforgiving—standards to themselves. Each slip-up is seen as an occasion for further self-indictment. Supporting this unhealthy attitude is the self-talk that plays through our hearts— messages often inherited from family and religious upbringing that reinforce hostile judgments about ourselves. In such a dysfunctional spirituality the gospel link between love of others and love of self is lost. Instead, we acknowledge that other people, however sinful, are to benefit from our compassion and forgiveness. But such indulgence need not be expended on ourselves.

Psychologist Kristin Neff has introduced the notion of self-compassion to remedy these self-punishing attitudes. She defines self-compassion as "an open-hearted way of relating to negative aspects of oneself and one's experiences that enables greater emotional resilience and psychological well-being." Self-compassion does not require us to deny our limitations or to refuse to recognize personal blunders and even sinful actions. Neff distinguishes self-compassion from psychology's earlier concentration on self-esteem, which quickly became identified with an uncritical attitude of "I'm OK; you're OK." Self-compassion does not encourage self-deception; it does forestall our automatic impulse to condemn ourselves.

Self-compassion is an exercise of gentle forgiveness, extending to ourselves the generous attitudes of understanding and leniency we are willing to offer to others. Neff traces the shape of this virtue in three dynamics. The first is a movement from self-judgment to self-kindness. We choose to turn away from harsh self-criticism and to avoid simplistic and hostile judgments about our own behavior. Here self-compassion resists the temptation to transform every mistake into further evidence that we are lazy, weak or simply a failure.

Self-compassion's second movement is from isolation toward a recognition of our common humanity. Self-compassion invites us back into the company of all humankind—both vulnerable and flawed. We are not alone as doer of misdeeds; rather, *we are all in this together*. Our frequent mistakes and even our occasional malice do not set us apart. Instead, these personal actions reflect our species' shared capacity for error and evil. This realization does not relieve us of responsibility for what we have done or from making a commitment to change our destructive behavior. But self-compassion invites us to bestow on ourselves the patience and benefit of the doubt that we would extend to others. Isolating ourselves from this wounded and wounding community and marking ourselves as deserving of special abuse support neither healing nor reconciliation.

Self-compassion's third dynamic moves from over-identification toward greater mindfulness. In over-identification we become absorbed and obsessed with each setback or mistake. The practice of mindfulness allows us to recognize our not-infrequent failures as part of a larger narrative: a life lived in grace and sin. We come to appreciate that our own journey alternates between generous actions and petty self-absorption. Attentive to this vulnerable state, we do not rush to judgment of our every mistake. Called to forgive others, we are willing also to forgive ourselves. Ready to show compassion to other fragile humans, we extend this comfort even to ourselves.

Practicing the Virtue of Self-Care

You must love the Lord your God with all your heart, with all your soul, with all your strength, and with all your mind, and your neighbor as yourself.

—Luke 10:27

This familiar text is often referred to as the two great commandments. In fact, we are urged here to honor three loving relationships—with God, with our neighbor and with ourselves. The link between love of self and love of others is confirmed from the psychological perspective as well. Studies consistently find that the attitudes and behaviors we display toward other people are closely related to the ways we respond to ourselves. People who love themselves are more accepting of their own strength and weaknesses, and they are likely to be gracious, generous and understanding in dealing with other people as well. People who are characteristically hard on others—severe in their judgments, impatient with other people's failures or mistakes or weakness—often respond to themselves in the same way. Both moral theologians and psychological therapists recognize the wider implications of self-acceptance and self-love. Psychologists discuss the significance of "post-narcissistic love of self"; pastoral guides call us to spiritual practices of self-care.

In *Virtues for Ordinary Christians* distinguished moral theologian James Keenan identifies virtues that are significant in contemporary Christian living. "Just as we have general responsibilities to everyone (justice), and special ones to particular persons (fidelity), so too we have a unique responsibility to ourselves (self-care)." A continuing tension in moral life is discernment—prudence—as we try to balance these several commitments. Keenan insists that self-care must "make its own claims" in these efforts of moral decision-making. Many of us—perhaps especially women—are influenced by religious and cultural ideals that promote selfless behavior in the service of other people's needs. Keenan recognizes both the value and the pressure of these expectations. He warns that without a strong commitment to the virtue of self-care, generous adults—both men and women—risk paying attention to their own needs only when time permits.

The practice of self-care is complicated for many women. These complications may also exist for men, particularly men with strong religious sensitivities and those in caregiving professions. Here we face one of the dilemmas of moral discernment—the relationship between care for self and care for others. In the complex lives of most adults, resolving this dilemma demands a critical reevaluation of earlier, often unstated, norms. The conventional socialization of many women, for example, has included ideals of generous devotion to the needs of others. These ideals gave priority to other people's needs; a "good" woman stands ready to defer, to overlook, even to sacrifice her own needs in order to respond to the practical and emotional demands of her network of family and friends.

Many women—and men—caught in these attitudes of self-denial gradually move toward a new awareness: *taking care of myself is as morally significant as taking care of other people.* This insight does not simplify personal decision-making. In fact, decisions often become more complicated, but also more mature. Moral consciousness at this level does not legitimize selfishness. But personal needs do not always and automatically take a back seat. Now when I am confronted by the needs of other people, a process of moral discernment begins. Generosity and altruistic concern remain significant. Family and work and civic responsibilities continue to make claims on me. Circumstances and situations still arise, in which I set aside my agenda or my needs or even my immediate well-being for the sake of other people. But now these actions are informed by judgment as well as generosity. My selfless response is not simply a foregone conclusion but the result of a moral choice.

Self-care is often a difficult virtue to embrace. Again Keenan encourages us, "The practice of self-care urges each person, through mercy, to enter into the deep chaos of one's own complicated life." And we are strengthened in this practice, as "we believe that the loving merciful light of Christ illuminates every dimension of the soul and helps us see what we need to do in the care of ourselves."

Compassion, then, is a cultivated grace. We often experience this movement of grace as a gift rather than simply a direct result of a personal decision. But we can dispose ourselves to this heartfelt response. Through formative and transformative practices we can strengthen this basic human capacity so that it becomes a reliable character strength.

10

Mood Swings in the Life of Faith

You have turned my mourning into dancing;
you have taken off my sackcloth and clothed
me with joy.

—Psalm 30

Mood swings are familiar companions on the journey of faith. Weeks of vigor and enthusiasm may give way to a time of distraction and fatigue. A season of self-confidence may shift into a period of self-doubt. We are surprised by a sudden surge of hope after months of struggle. Though these emotional shifts are interior, we know they are shaped by the changing moods of family, nation and religious heritage. It should come as no surprise that the Christian tradition itself has experienced mood swings in its long history.

In the Beginning

Our Hebrew ancestors unashamedly laced their prayers with emotion. Powerful feelings—positive and painful—were the fuel of their passionate relationship with Yahweh. In a time of great distress they could pray, with Job, "Now that I have lost all taste for life I will give free rein to my complaints; I will let my embittered soul speak out" (Jb 7:11). In periods of celebration they would pray, "I will give thanks to the Lord with my whole heart . . . I will sing praise to your name, O Most High" (Ps 9:1, 2).The decline of old age would evoke an emotional plea: "O Lord, do not desert me now that I am old and gray" (Ps 71).

The psalms display a full range of emotions. "Clap your hands, all you peoples; shout to God with loud songs of joy for the Lord, the Most High, is awesome" (Ps 4). Throughout we meet sentiments of

97

gladness, delight, rejoicing. "You show me the path of life. In your presence there is fullness of joy. In your right hand are pleasures evermore" (Ps 16). But most psalms (written, biblical scholars suggest, during the time of Israel's exile) are cries of lament in which feelings of guilt, shame, grief, regret and loneliness tumble out in rapid succession. "I am weary with my moaning . . . My eyes waste away because of grief" (Ps 7); "My God, my God, why have you forsaken me? Why are you so far from helping me, from the words of my groaning?" (Ps 22). But typically, this cavalcade of painful feelings is followed by a sudden shift: "You have turned my mourning into dancing" (Ps 30:11).

Every possible feeling, however painful or pleasurable, turned the Israelites toward their merciful God. No feeling—anger, sorrow, fear, despair—was excluded from their intimate and combative relationship with Yahweh. Painful emotions seemed to connect them with their God, if only to remind them of their own fickle faith. Perhaps their comfort with strong feelings reflected the range of emotions they discovered within the Creator: "Yahweh is tender and compassionate; slow to anger, most loving. God's indignation does not last forever, God's resentment exists only a short time" (Ps 103). Abraham Heschel reminds us that anger and compassion are the mood swings in the heart of God.

Israel's recognition of mood swings in the life of Yahweh was reflected in powerful shifts in their own destiny. Exhilaration at their escape from slavery in Egypt was soon replaced by the bewilderment of decades in the desert. Satisfaction at reaching "the land flowing with milk and honey" was eventually displaced by the despair accompanying their exile in Babylon. Profound humility before their mysterious God was matched by the boldness with which they approached Yahweh in both praise and rebuke. Through these cycles Yahweh's chosen people became familiar with emotional extremes as they turned every emotion into prayer.

This wholehearted embrace of emotions continues into the New Testament. The Gospels portray Jesus as more than "meek and humble of heart"; he is frequently moved by anger, sadness and even regret. In his many letters to the early Christian communities Paul also displayed a range of emotions. Writing to those in Corinth, he exclaimed: "I am filled with consolation and am overjoyed even in my afflictions" (2 Cor 7:4). And the earthy spirituality so abundant in the Hebrew scriptures was still very much alive for Paul. He could write of "all creation groaning in labor pains until now . . . We groan inwardly as we wait for adoption, the redemption of our bodies." And he would describe the healing power of the Holy Spirit when "we do not know how to pray. [Then] that very Spirit intercedes for us in sighs too deep for words" (Rom 8:22; 8:26). Groans and sighs were accepted as wordless expressions of prayer.

A Mood Swing in Early Christianity

Paul's instructions to these new communities of faith also included a more cautious attitude. Struggling to excite these new believers toward a deepening faith, Paul crafted a dichotomy between flesh and spirit. "Spirit," for Paul, pointed to the more generous aspects of our humanity, those movements more closely aligned to the full humanity of the risen Christ. Paul used "flesh" as a metaphor, referring less to human embodiment than to those selfish impulses that turn humans away from God and from our own deepest values. Over time, however, many Christians came to interpret the term *flesh* literally, as identifying all aspects of our physical existence. Then emotional life—rooted in the body and responding to its needs—seemed destined to be in tension with humanity's higher destiny. "Nothing good dwells within me, that is, in my flesh." (Rom 7:18). Passages from John's Gospel reinforce this view: "It is the spirit that gives life; the flesh is useless" (Jn 6:63).

At the end of the fourth century, as we have seen, Augustine crafted a spirituality that indicted both pleasure and desire. His convictions were to become authoritative in Western Christianity for the next six hundred years. In his autobiography Augustine reveals that the pleasure that accompanied eating and drinking were a constant source of concern. He writes that, in eating, "a dangerous pleasure" accompanies this necessary exercise in nourishment. He would prefer to take food and drink "as medicine," stripped of their pleasure. For Augustine, the pleasures of sight were another source of temptation: "sense experience in general is called concupiscence of the eyes" (*The Confessions* 10.35). He is wary of "glowing and beautiful colors. These things must not take hold on my soul; that is for God to do."

If pleasure is dangerous for Augustine, desire is deceptive. Original sin has distorted human desire, reshaping it as lust. This wound leaves desire an irrational and unreliable movement in Christian life. Beautiful sights and sounds and tastes are more likely to distract us, even seduce us, than to lead us to God.

Augustine's attitude toward laughter offers a touching example of his discomfort with emotional arousals. He seems unable to appreciate humor's power to refresh the spirit and even heal the heart. In his judgment, laughter is most often used for ridicule or derision . . . a judgment rooted in his own memories of being insulted and mocked. For Augustine, laughter, held hostage by shame, could not serve as a medium of shared delight.

This growing bias against emotions was not shared by all communities within the early church. Gregory of Nyssa, a contemporary of Augustine who ministered within the church of the East (Turkey), crafted an optimistic spirituality rooted in the human desire for God. The image of God's indwelling the human soul was, for Gregory, a dynamic source. God's image within us triggers the desire to return to our Source. So for Gregory, desire in its first instance is a vital God-given force. Human sinfulness did not render desire utterly suspect, as in Augustine's view. The longings we experience in everyday life echo the Creator's desire for our very existence.

In a dazzling passage Gregory links love and desire: "Because Wisdom is speaking, love with all your heart and with all your strength (Dt 6:5), as much as you can. Desire as much as possible. And to these words I boldly add, fall in love [*eros*]!" "This passion," Gregory continues, "is without reproach and dispassionate, as Wisdom says in Proverbs when she enjoins us to fall in love [*eros*] with divine Beauty." Peter Brown reminds us that Gregory's pastoral concern was much less focused on sexual temptation than on "the tragic roots of pride, avarice, and family honor" that were likely to distract the Christian living in the world.

The Great Schism in the eleventh century split Eastern and Western Christianity. As a result, Gregory's optimistic vision of the emotions in Christian spirituality was lost to the Western Church. Instead, a profound hesitance regarding the emotions continued, leading to what one church historian has called a certain patristic reserve.

Mood Swings in the Life of Faith

For nearly a millennium spiritual detachment from the emotions continued to shape Christian spirituality in the West. During these centuries devotion to the crucified Jesus was virtually unknown. Byzantine icons, for example, characteristically depicted Christ triumphant on a glorious cross, with no painful emotions on display. For reasons we do not fully understand, a powerful shift in piety and devotion occurred in Europe around the twelfth century. This shift might itself be described as a mood swing in the faith life of Christian communities.

The work of the artist Cimabue in the thirteenth century provides a striking symbol of this shift. Best known as the teacher of Giotto,

Cimabue stands at the watershed where Byzantine art, with its cool and detached beauty, gives way to the early Renaissance and its fascination with the body. The Byzantine cross, often gilded and adorned with precious stones, was an object of exaltation, not an instrument of torture. Christ's wounds were glorious rather than gruesome; his body was upright and triumphant. Cimabue brought different emotions into his depiction of the cross. Here we see the human portrait of a man whose body is twisted in pain.

In this same period Francis of Assisi was crafting a down-to-earth spirituality. Franciscan spirituality is emphatically affective; Francis's devotion to the humanity of Jesus honored all the emotions expressed in his painful passion and death. In this same century the body of Jesus received special attention in the annual celebration of the feast of Corpus Christi. In the fourteenth century the lay-led piety movement Devotio Moderna emphasized an intense personal relationship with Jesus. In these novel expressions of Christian devotion, emotion became the very medium of faith.

Thomas Aquinas added his voice in support of this new appreciation of the emotions when he argued, against Augustine, that "moral virtues cannot be without passion." In his theology Aquinas reunited the body and its passions with the soul and its virtues. Charles Taylor identifies this movement as "a devout humanism" in which emotions and faith embraced with vigor.

The High Renaissance in the sixteenth century displayed this emotion-filled embodied spirituality in its most graphic detail. Michelangelo's "Pieta" and Bernini's "Theresa in Ecstasy" portrayed flesh and spirit in vigorous embrace. In the *Spiritual Exercises* Ignatius Loyola urged retreatants to imagine, in full emotional detail, the scriptural scene on which one was meditating in order to *feel* God's presence. John of the Cross and Teresa of Avila evoked erotic imagery to describe the desire for God. This enthusiastic embrace of the body and all its emotions was not to last long. Profound movements of religious reform, emerging from both Protestant and Catholic sources in the sixteenth century, would leave little room for emotion's disruptive influence.

An "Excarnation"

Martin Luther, a chief architect of the Protestant Reformation, followed Augustine in his judgment of the bitter fruit of original sin: human nature, now broken, was no longer reliable as guide in a life of faith. Movements of the heart and stirrings of the body are not to be trusted. John Calvin expanded this negative evaluation: human nature is totally depraved. John Wesley, founder of Methodism, wrote explicitly of the mayhem that the emotions brought to a life of faith: "Grief and anger and hatred and fear and shame at once rushed in upon it [the will]; the whole train of earthly, sensual and devilish passions fastened on and tore it to pieces." From this point forward, both Protestants and Catholics developed spiritualities that further emphasized a suspicion of emotion.

As Reform Christians emptied their churches of incense and candles and images of saints, Catholics restructured many of their own ritual practices. The sacramental bread of the Eucharist, once provided by home ovens, was now restricted to tasteless white wafers, the more to represent *panis angelicus* (the bread of angels). Baptism, once a ritual of full immersion and sensual oils, was reduced to a ritual trickle of water poured over the forehead. Charles Taylor refers to this stripping away of sensuality as the historical "excarnation" in Christian life: "the transfer of our religious life out of bodily forms of ritual, worship, practice, so that it comes more and more to reside *in the head*." This shift moves faith away from its incarnational roots. "Christianity, as the faith of the Incarnate God, is denying something essential to itself as long as it remains wedded to forms which excarnate."

Catholic moral theology, still in its formative years at this point, adopted a rationalistic approach to ethics in its search for universal principles to provide certitude to its moral convictions. The more imaginative and adventurous theological method of Aquinas and others in the late medieval world gave way to a more carefully censored approach. Stephen Toulmin describes a shift from "free-wheeling *summas* to centrally authorized *manuals*."

Major exceptions to this rationalistic trend were the Baroque movement in church architecture and a surge of emotional piety in the sixteenth and seventeenth centuries. New Catholic churches were designed in a style that favored theatrical interiors, with the sanctuary arranged as a stage, and complemented with multiple ornate sculptures. Growing interest at this time in devotions to the body of Christ—feasts dedicated to the Sacred Heart and to the Precious Blood—marked a distinctive surge in a newly emotional piety.

In the wider culture of seventeenth-century Enlightenment Europe, philosophical and scientific developments supported a deepening dualism of reason and emotion. Descartes grounded philosophy itself in a rational certitude: "I think, therefore I am." For him and many who followed his philosophical lead, only thought could guarantee an objective, knowable reality. Rationality came to define human identity; this sole trustworthy resource stood apart from the body and its many unreliable feelings.

Religious knowing was a major casualty of this divorce of reason and emotion. In the face of logical procedures and rational analysis, the moral intuitions and ritual expressions of religion suddenly seemed—at least to the intellectuals of the time—to be unreliable guides to truth. Reason alone was judged capable of delivering trustworthy access to the world. Artistic expression and religious methods of apprehending truth became suspect, judged to be too emotional or even irrational.

In defense of the faith, theologians threw up a wall between reason and faith. Reality, as now imagined, seemed divided between *nature*—the measurable world that was now ceded to science and reason—and the *supernatural*—a realm of religious belief safely separated from the prying eyes of scientists. This dualism exacted a high price: religious faith was rescued from secular scrutiny, but only by leaving this world. For many believers faith would become disconnected from everyday experience, replaced by an intellectual assent to certain eternal *truths*.

By the middle of the twentieth century, Western culture's confidence in reason was wearing thin. Rational planning and advanced technology had increased the efficiency of the death camps in Europe; scientific research had developed weapons capable of destroying hundreds of thousand of lives in two days in Japan. The myth of endless progress driven by reason and science proved false, leaving space for a shift in attitudes toward emotions.

In the course of the twentieth century the emotions became significant again in both the human sciences and in theological study. Biblical scholars became more respectful of the role of feeling in these sacred texts, rediscovering the passionate prayer of the Book of Psalms, the emotional cries of grief in the Book of Lamentations. Christians found again in the gospel stories a portrait of Jesus as a man of feeling, familiar with a full range of humanity's distressing emotions. There was a growing recognition that ours is not a dispassionate Divinity, but a God of desire. Returning passion to the heart of God has authorized a recovery of the emotions as allies on the spiritual journey. This welcoming of emotions has, in turn, opened spirituality to a more wholehearted embrace of the vulnerability that defines our humanness.

Vulnerability and Christian Faith

"Human beings are deeply troubled about being human—about being highly intelligent and resourceful, on the one hand, but weak and vulnerable, helpless against death, on the other. We are ashamed of this awkward condition and, in manifold ways, we try to hide from it." Martha Nussbaum, in her aptly titled *Hiding from Humanity*, traces the intimate links between our emotional life and vulnerability. We are made uneasy in the face of the anxiety, fear and shame that arise with some regularity on the human journey. But this vulnerability "is inseparable both from our sociability, and from our propensity to emotional attachment." Reminding us that the often distressing "emotions of compassion, grief, fear, and anger are . . . essential and valuable reminders of our common humanity," Nussbaum concludes: "Emotions are thus, in effect, acknowledgments of neediness and lack of self-sufficiency."

For our religious ancestors in ancient Israel, vulnerability defined every relationship with God: memories of their lives as slaves; recollections of the frightening vulnerability of the desert; the sense of impotence while in exile. Vulnerability, and the emotions it evoked, was the very medium of their religious faith.

This religious embrace of vulnerability came under fire in the early centuries of Christian history. In the culture where Christian faith was taking shape, Stoic commitments to self-sufficiency led to a severing of bodily needs from human dignity. "Need itself does not have dignity . . . We do not think of the hunger of the body, its need for shelter, for care in time of illness, and for love, as among the ingredients of its dignity." Seneca, writing in Rome in the first century, described an ideal of rational self-sufficiency that outlawed any surrender to passion. For him and other Stoics emotional vulnerability arose only as a weakness.

In this same period Christian theologians were eager to describe their God as equal to the philosophical standards of the time. To do this they departed from their scriptural heritage and described their God as impassible—beyond the sway of all emotions, transcendently removed from the feelings that render humans so weak and vulnerable. Elizabeth Johnson describes this development: "Possessing all perfections in an unimaginable way, the divine nature has no possibility for change, cannot be affected by the world, and, of course, cannot suffer . . . The ideal for human beings is likewise a self-conquest that will enable people to control their passions and dwell in an untroubled realm of spirit."

But even as this new ideal was being forged, memories from scripture endured: recollections of Yahweh so in love with creation that God was moved with regret (Gn 6), frequently angered (Ps 7) and even made jealous (Ex 20). The incarnation represented the greatest scandal, with its claim that God became flesh, to be made vulnerable in the endless ways familiar to mortals. Further, this vulnerability was on painful display in the passion and death of Jesus. How could this be? Doesn't the life of Jesus force us to see vulnerability as more than weakness? Could vulnerability even be seen as holy, as something to be cherished among those who follow Christ?

Many Christians today bring to our spiritual journey our humble experiences of vulnerability: the dramatic needs of our small children for every kind of nurture; the needs of beloved partners that do not distance us from each other, but only draw us closer. And we continue to explore the ways in which our weakness may be more blessing than curse, how even our vulnerability may be a signature gift of these mortal bodies that are created in the image of God.

We may expect these mood swings in the life of faith to continue. Meanwhile, shaped by the visceral emotions on display in the scriptures and following Jesus, who was beset with every kind of emotion, we forge our spiritual path in this season of the church's life.

PART III

RELIGIOUS EMOTIONS

No human emotion belongs uniquely to religion, but powerful feelings appear repeatedly in religious traditions, serving as doorways to the sacred.

Faith, hope and charity begin their life as fragile feelings and gradually mature, through many reversals, into reliable resources that ground a life of Christian faith.

The rhythm of gratitude and generosity, both moral emotions and Christian virtues, gives shape to our maturing lives.

The evolved capacities of justice and mercy arise as instinctive responses to suffering and injustice, then grow into essential guides on the journey of faith.

We conclude our exploration of the healing emotions with a reflection on religion and the expansive ways of knowing opened up by emotion and intuition.

11

Ennobling Passions—
Faith, Hope and Charity

Now faith, love and hope abide, these three;
and the greatest of these is love.
—1 CORINTHIANS 13:13

Enduring invitations run through our lives: to put our trust in the living God as the mysterious source of life; to lean expectantly toward a future that may yield blessings we ourselves cannot produce; to expand our loving concern to include all those crafted in the image of God. The Christian tradition has named these spiritual resources as the core virtues of faith, hope and charity.

In the dualism that still haunts our religious heritage, these virtues came to be identified as *infused,* that is, given to us solely through the action of the Holy Spirit. This terminology was meant to distinguish these graces—and perhaps to distance them—from virtuous habits that might be acquired through our own effort. As infused, these virtues were free of the emotional swings and shifting moods of an embodied existence. But this disconnect had disappointing results. The focus of faith shifted, and passionate attachment to God was replaced by mental assent to revealed truths. Hope became an abiding confidence in personal salvation, purged of all doubt or hesitance. Charity supported a pious concern for those in need, which was often oblivious to the unjust social structures that defeat so many human lives.

Aquinas, as we have seen, made a startling departure from the earlier tradition's uncoupling of virtue from passion. Convinced that virtue itself rides on the energy of passion, Aquinas drew a distinction that would shape subsequent theological discussion. "If by passions we mean inordinate affections, as the Stoics held, then it is clear that perfect virtue is without passions. But if by passions we mean all

movements of sense appetite, then it is plain that the moral virtues
. . . cannot be without the passions; virtue produces orderly passions." Virtues, Aquinas insisted, do not suppress passions but shape
their vitality for noble purposes. Following this insight, Christian life
becomes a passionate vocation.

Taking his cue from Aquinas, contemporary philosopher Roberto
Unger has reclaimed the virtues of faith, hope and charity as "ennobling passions." Unger offers a holistic portrait of human life in which
reason and passion work as partners. The distinct contribution of the
passions in this relationship is to provide vital resources that reason
alone cannot summon. Passion serves "as an elementary energy without which reason would be impotent and aimless." Unger traces the
limits of reason: "Though reason gives us knowledge of the world, it
does not tell us in the final instance what to want and what to do. It
cannot provide the quality of sustained commitment." Passion opens
us to realities we might otherwise never experience: "There are some
revelations into our and other people's humanity that we achieve
only through experience of passion." Spiritual insight, then, is not a
mystical event that is disconnected from our bodily lives. Our deepest knowing arises in the passionate links that bind us to one another
and to God.

Christian Virtues as Ennobling Passions

The core virtues of faith, hope and charity are religious passions;
they support our wholehearted investment in full and flourishing
lives. Religious faith is a passionate clinging to God, even in the face
of cultural forces that ignore or reject such devotion. Religious hope
describes our often fragile conviction that, despite the malice and injustice that stalk our world, God will prevail. Religious love expands
our commitment to embrace those who are neglected or rejected by
society. In Unger's vision these core Christian virtues are passionate
ways of encountering the Mystery that remains forever beyond our
reach.

Unger believes that these passionate engagements have the power
to *ennoble* our lives. Daring to entrust our lives to others, willing to
expect blessings and healing, eager to extend our love even to those
so different from ourselves—these risky actions render our lives more
expansive and more generous. These virtuous passions are also *transformative*, harboring the ability "to penetrate the crust of everyday
perception and habit." They display the broaden-and-build dynamic
described by Barbara Fredrickson. "The career of faith, hope and love

. . . may decisively enlarge the area of social life in which human reconciliation can take hold and human freedom can be acknowledged."

The Ennobling Passion of Faith

"Every act of love implies an act of faith." To love others we must be willing to open ourselves to them. But how can we justify this risky vulnerability? As Unger starkly suggests, "If someone challenged you to show that you were justified in undertaking the risk, you could not do so." Faith in God is similar: "To have faith in God is to put oneself in His hands, with nothing to go on but the ambiguous signs of His presence in the world and His intervention in history." Unger acknowledges the full sweep of this audacious passion, as it leads us to invest our future in relationships that we cannot control.

The ennobling passion of faith is evident in the actions of our religious ancestors in the desert and later in exile; despite evidence to the contrary, they clung to a conviction that Yahweh would lead them to a better life. Faith is the ennobling passion we see in Jesus as he prays in anguish in the garden, struggling to face his future. In our own day faith appears in the extraordinary strength that allows us to cling to our faithful God, even in the midst of a personal tragedy. Unger links faith with the response of trust: "The motive to trust is my confidence that, whatever the temporary disappointments and misunderstandings, the others will not abandon me in the long run."

Psychologist Erik Erikson has explored trust as an essential human capacity: "By *trust* I mean an essential trustfulness of others as well as a fundamental sense of one's own trustworthiness." Erikson then links trust with religious faith. "Trust, then, becomes the capacity for faith—a vital need for which man must find some institutional confirmation. Religion, it seems, is the oldest and has been the most lasting institution to serve the ritual restoration of a sense of trust in the form of faith." This dynamic of trust, rooted in a maturing faith, is itself an ennobling passion.

The Ennobling Passion of Hope

"Hope, like faith, represents an extension and deepening of love," writes Unger. And this passion has its special ennobling effect: "A person's hope enables him to undertake the experimental lifting of defenses that love requires." Hope often appears more as a fragile gift than a sure possession. We begin to hope in the midst of a threatening situation; we are not sure where this emotion and grace come from. "Now hope that is seen is not hope for who hopes for what is seen?

But if we hope for what we do not see, we wait in patience" (Rom 8:24).

Unger identifies hope as an uninvited envoy, bringing visions and options of what tomorrow might look like. Often arriving as surprise, this passion sees a way through conflicts and barriers that had, a moment before, seemed impregnable. Hope, for Unger, is an *ennobling* passion because it awakens us to possibilities that will render our own lives more expansive, more generous.

Hope is a *transformative* power. It carries the potential to change our present, to heal our past and to foresee and craft a future we had previously not anticipated. Hope allows us to see through the present, the binding force of the status quo and the received wisdom that the current arrangement of society or self is the way things have to be.

Present circumstances and prevailing structures—in world politics, in the national economy or in our own families—can exercise a tyranny and lock us into socially prescribed behaviors. The passion of hope "loosens the hold that routines or character exercise over the imagination."

Hope can likewise alter the past. Each of us has learned that the past is over and finished; we cannot undo the "spilled milk" of our mistakes. Our culture encourages us, whatever our failings or regrets, to put it behind us and move on. If we are fortunate we may later learn that the past is *not* over because it has not finished with us. It survives in unhealed wounds, inherited fears and unquenched desires for revenge. Hope rallies us against this fatalism, giving us "the ability to downgrade the influence of past and present structure and compulsions."

The transformative power of hope is especially addressed to the future. Through the gift and grace of hope we can imagine that the future is not simply "more of the same." We are now able to picture our own future in more generous ways. Just as hope challenges the finality of the past, so it questions the fatalism of the future. Hope says that it need not be so. This ennobling passion awakens in us extravagant dreams, visions of a society and self that do not yet exist.

Hope supports the promises through which we build bridges to an unforeseeable future. George Steiner writes of the hope that underlies all language: confidence that our words and our worlds are connected; trust that our exchanges with one another are reliable. With language we create webs of connection and meaning; we build bonds to which we become answerable, responsible. From this hopeful exchange all our commitments and covenants arise.

Appreciating this ennobling passion deepens as we recall our mood when hope drains from our life. As depression or despair overwhelm us, we lose confidence in the future. With this passion gone, we begin to lose our way. We cannot see "a way through" that will lead us to life in abundance.

The Ennobling Passion of Love

Love is always surprising. This ennobling impulse draws us out of self-protective privacy to approach another person. This movement, fraught with vulnerability, "always has something of the miraculous," Unger insists. "It is an act of grace devoid of condescension or resentment."

But even as grace, genuine love enlists us in extraordinary maneuvers. As lovers, we "run the risk of being rebuffed or disappointed." We expose ourselves to "perilous emotion and ridiculous gesture." But as love frees itself from illusion, this virtuous passion steadies us through the ups and downs of actual relationships. Once delivered from romantic and idealistic distortions, love invites us "toward the acceptance of the beloved as defective, ambiguous, original reality."

Unger explores *sympathy* as the foundation of the passionate virtue of love. Sympathy "serves as *the* ennobling passion—less a passion than the moral capability supporting the entire life of the passions." Sympathy allows us to recognize in the vulnerability of the other person the brokenness we all share. This recognition draws us toward others in sympathetic care.

Passion Gone Astray

Love's passion sometimes misfires. Two common experiences—lust and jealousy—squander love's nobility. Unger describes lust as "sexual attraction untransformed by love and . . . uninspired by the imagination of otherness." When sexual attraction degenerates into lust, we "attempt to reduce others to the condition of mere occasions for the enjoyment of solitary pleasures." The risks of love are set aside in favor of a safer search for a private delight. Paul Ricoeur describes lust in the idiom of *eroticism*, defining this term as "a restless desire for pleasure" disengaged from any "lasting and intimate interpersonal bond." When tenderness is displaced by eroticism, "an egoistic cultivation of pleasure wins out over mutual exchange."

In jealousy, love's nobility is squandered as well. Here the gift of passion becomes competitive, since "the formative image of jealousy is always one of property or possession." Our longing for a deepened relationship with the beloved transforms our vision; all others are now seen as threats and intruders. This desire to possess—to take the beloved *out of circulation*—guarantees defeat of the free gift of love.

Honoring the Religious Imagination

Behold, I am doing a new thing. Now it breaks forth. Do you not perceive it?

—ISAIAH 43:19

Unger challenges us to restore these ennobling virtues to our embodied selves. But many of us have been instructed to view these virtues as abiding in our intellect and will, safely separated from the hormonal surges of strong emotion. So recognizing the core virtues of faith, hope and charity as ennobling passions requires a strong imagination.

The capacity of imagination enables us to reflect on "what does not (yet) exist." Psychologist Daniel Gilbert describes this evolved capacity: "The greatest achievement of the human brain is its ability to imagine objects and episodes that do not exist in the realm of the real, and it is this ability that allows us to think about the future. If nature has given us a greater gift, no one has named it."

In Christian history the imagination was often castigated as the source of sexual temptations; here erotic dreams, waking and sleeping, had their source. It was also in the imagination that people played out fantasies of violence—striking back at an enemy or cruelly punishing an adversary. Thus did this interior resource seem to merit its negative reputation. But in recent psychological and theological discussion, imagination has been recovered as powerful resource, waiting to be cultivated in support of our best hopes and deepest values.

Faith: Re-Imagining Our World

Religious faith is a way of imagining the world. Recognizing that our world was created by and is now sustained by a loving Creator, who is present yet invisible, takes a well-developed imagination. This is not to suggest that religious faith is a fantasy or a mere figment of our mind. It is to recognize that faith is a God-given ability to envision the world.

Our religious ancestors, having escaped slavery in Egypt, found themselves lost in the desert. In this threatening setting some began to dream of "a land flowing with milk and honey." This ideal existed first only in their imaginations, fevered perhaps by the desert heat. But this hope would become a reality. Living in exile in Babylon centuries later, the Jews had lost heart, unable to imagine any rescue from this wretched existence. But the prophet Isaiah foresaw a dramatic change, proclaiming that God would lead this defeated people out of exile and back to their land and language and Temple. This rescue existed first only in imagination. This same prophet also envisioned a future time when "swords would be beaten into plowshares" (Is 2:4). This dreamlike hope, unlikely then and now, still stirs the imaginations of peace makers today.

Walter Brueggemann describes biblical revelation as "an act of faithful imagination" that offers us "a wondrously demanding alternative to the world that is immediately and visibly at hand." As Christians read biblical accounts of suffering and surprising graces, our imaginations are invited to embrace a particular vision of the world. William Spohn suggests that these powerful stories "tutor the imagination." The Bible, he argues, does not give us explicit instructions for resolving the moral dilemmas we face. Instead, its stories and symbols "encourage certain scenarios." These vivid accounts—Jesus' welcome of sinners and strangers, his instruction to forgive seventy times seven, his fidelity to his Father's will—evoke our own response. We return to these stories again and again, bathing our imaginations in a particular vision of reality. The role of the Bible, with its dramatic parables and compelling images, is to shape our imagination and motivate us "to go and do likewise."

Hope: Envisioning the Reign of God

At the outset of his mission Jesus proclaimed the reign of God was at hand. He announced a new era in human history—a time of justice and love. Later, when challenged by others to give evidence of this vision of a better world, Jesus assured his listeners that "the reign of God is among you" (Lk 17:21). But his listeners might well have wondered: where exactly is this godly reign, this kingdom? Jesus seemed to insist that this longed-for reality was already present among them—perhaps not yet in actual fact but in their hopeful imaginations. The reign of God names a transformed way of life that we must first be able to imagine; only then can it become the reality that, with God's help, we set out to craft.

Experience on every side testifies to the enduring reality of injustice, violence and poverty. The evidence is so pervasive that we are tempted to say that nothing can be done. But the small voice of the religious imagination, tutored by biblical testimonies, whispers that "it could be otherwise." And our hope is born again.

Theologian Monika Hellwig reinforces the public and communal dimension of biblical hope:

> To hope seriously for the coming reign of God means to reorder not only immediate individual relationships in justice, charity and compassion, but also those larger structures or patterns of relationships among us that determine whether people live or starve, whether they can live humanly or are brutalized, whether they can participate in community or are excluded, whether their lives are an experience of the gracious goodness of the creator or are lived in torture and constant fear.

She then draws out the inevitable conclusion: "The reign of God as the promised goal of Christian life and hope necessarily has a this-worldly, public dimension."

The Bible tutors our imagination, so that we begin to perceive a way of life cleansed of enmity and revenge. In this vision strangers and aliens are recognized as brothers and sisters. Daring to imagine such a world, we are moved to realize this interior hope in new patterns of social life.

Charity: Re-imagining the Other

> *A crowd was sitting around him, and they said*
> *to him, "Your mother and your brothers and sis-*
> *ters are outside, asking for you." And he replied,*
> *"Who are my mother and my brothers?*
>
> —MARK 3:32

Jesus was constantly challenging the boundaries of belonging. He questioned the rigid bloodlines that separated tribe from tribe and judged strangers to stand outside "our" group's concern. Jesus seemed always to be expanding the definition of who belongs. His example invites us to imagine our social world in new ways, extending mutual support and accountability beyond the constraints of family lines and tribal loyalty.

Jesus' welcoming stance resonates with themes in the Hebrew bible. Here the stranger often appears as a vehicle of revelation. The crucial revelation to Abraham that initiates the history of salvation for Jews and Christians is linked to the appearance of "three strangers" (Gn 18). Later in this same biblical text Jacob wrestles in the dark with an anonymous force—a stranger whom, by daylight, he will recognize as his God (Gn 32). The message is repeated and clear: God comes to us through strangers. Our rigid and well-learned biases toward aliens and outsiders are challenged in the face of this revelation.

The most dramatic New Testament story about the stranger appears toward the end of Luke's Gospel. Two disciples are trudging home to the city of Emmaus, grief-stricken after the death of Jesus. They are joined by someone they do not recognize. This stranger questions them about their distress, then reminds them of the prophets' teaching that life comes from death. Reaching their home the two invite the stranger to join them for dinner. And in the breaking of the bread they recognize the stranger as Christ. Then, curiously, Jesus immediately disappears. The recognition has been like a flash—a sudden epiphany.

This story calls us to recognize in the stranger the presence of Christ. But this recognition, like any act of faith, requires a good imagination. The story of Emmaus moves us today because we too have recognized in blessed moments—our imaginations having been tutored by this story—that the stranger, the resident alien or vulnerable outsider, has the face of Christ.

12

Gratitude and Generosity

Give and it will be given to you; a good measure,
pressed down, shaken together, running over,
will be put in your lap.

—LUKE 6:38

A friend's small gift takes us by surprise. The item itself is inexpensive, but the gesture is generous and totally unexpected. We are delighted, moved by both pleasure and affection. Some invisible bond between us, already in place, grows stronger. Elsewhere in our lives, too, gratitude responds to the unanticipated gifts and good fortune that come our way. And we are drawn in two directions: to give thanks to those who have favored us and, in turn, to share with others through our own acts of generosity. As Lewis Hyde writes, "The labor of gratitude is generosity."

Gratitude is a moral emotion, laying down patterns of giving and receiving that establish our social world. As these mutual exchanges reinforce trust, reliable relationships blossom. Feeling grateful reflects essential moral instincts: to acknowledge our dependence, to honor our indebtedness, to appreciate the benefactors with whom we are inextricably linked.

Margaret Visser links gratitude with awe: "Deeply felt gratefulness is a species of awe, and as such requires humility. It implies a sense of one's littleness before the wonder of the universe, of the earth and all of nature, of one's own life—and before the goodness of others." She concludes: "Gratitude, like awe, is the opposite of what we call 'taking things for granted,' which is receiving and not seeing why one should be grateful . . . Gratitude, like awe, is a matter of looking, and ultimately of insight."

Memory is the natural habitat of gratitude. We recall the gifts we have received, and we give thanks. We savor our connections with those who have cared for and protected and encouraged us. Sociologist Georg Simmel has described gratitude as "a kind of moral memory of mankind that binds together those who have exchanged gifts." Gratitude is an arousal that keeps community alive.

Emerging spontaneously in the flow of favors, gratitude expands over time into an enduring mood. Visser describes this mood as a *cultivated disposition:* "one is in some sense grateful *in advance* of any gift or favor, because one is prepared to recognize goodness and be grateful for it." Like other moral dispositions, gratitude can be nurtured and expressed through spiritual practice: our intentional expressions of thanks to those who have enriched our lives. Through such regular practice, this moral emotion deepens into virtue.

Gratitude is widely recognized as a religious emotion. The claim here is not that thanksgiving is restricted to institutional religion. But giving thanks often draws our attention to sources beyond here and now. Some benefits received evoke our awareness of blessings bestowed. Here we resonate with Lewis Hyde's conviction: "A circulation of gifts nourishes those parts of our spirit that are not entirely personal, parts that derive from nature, the group, the race, or the gods." This realization leads many of us to voice our appreciation in prayer.

At the core of Christian life lies the *saving rhythm* of giving and receiving. Learning to be grateful for all we have received rescues us from pettiness, resentment and a chronic sense of entitlement. Learning to be generous with our resources frees us from worry, hoarding and selfishness. In these movements of gratitude and generosity, our lives will flourish.

Gratitude is central in liturgical celebration. We gather to give thanks for the extravagance of creation and for the continuing outpouring of God's gifts. At the feasts of Passover and Easter we praise God for delivery from slavery and for the promise of freedom. The most significant liturgical action of the Christian community is the celebration of *eucharist,* literally, "thanksgiving."

As gratitude thrives within a community of faith, this gathering serves as a school of the emotions. Here we are formed by ceremonies of praise and rituals of thanksgiving. Here we learn that life itself comes unearned, a gift to be cherished for as long as it is given. Here we are made aware of the endless bounty that has come our way—from daily breath and bread, to faithful companions, to the talents and abilities with which we have been gifted. In these communities we are introduced to the sacred alchemy of gift giving. In the words of Lewis Hyde, "We are enlightened when our gifts rise from pools we cannot fathom. Then we know they are not a solitary egoism and they are inexhaustible . . . When the gift passes out of sight and then returns, we are enlivened."

The Good Gift

But not all that we are given comes as a true gift. Some kinds of giving bind in an indebtedness that cripples us; others entrap us in a demeaning dependency. Here we are diminished rather than enlivened. A false gift carries a hidden price. Accepting the donation, we find ourselves obligated to the giver. Sometimes the gift comes as a "reward." Only later do we see that the reward is meant to be an incentive, urging us to become partner to someone else's plans. What is given comes not from generosity but from a desire to control. Gift giving can be perverted in ways that turn gratitude into servitude. The seemingly harmless aspiration of parents or teachers that those in their care will "make us proud" often ends in injury to all parties. A young person labors valiantly to please, to be worthy of the benefits received. In this setting gratitude is measured in meeting someone else's expectations.

A good gift is "a yoke that is sweet and a burden that is light." It is given not to extract our dependence or even to elicit gratitude. Freely given, a good gift sets us free. Without hidden hooks it does not bind us to the giver's agenda. The genuine gift, let go by the giver, becomes truly ours. We remember where the gift comes from, but this memory does not enslave us or inhibit our own effort to hand on the gift.

The good gift also sets us free from fear, opening us to the world's mysterious and inexhaustible abundance. We learn that we have an endless potential to support life and to respond with generosity. Most mysterious of all, we find that our giving does not deplete us. But this extraordinary realization—in "losing" the gift I am not diminished—is constantly threatened by an opposing claim that another's gain is our loss. With this conviction we must cling to what we have. We need to hoard our goods and defend our supplies. If we give anything we must receive adequate compensation. Fear acts like a fierce watchdog. Keenly aware of threatening scarcity and the perils of supply and demand, we keep checking our larder or our bank account. A genuine gift reinforces a different vision. The gospel proclamation that "perfect love casts out fear" echoes in the conviction that the good gift casts out fear.

A good gift rescues us from loneliness. This mood of isolation often occurs when we wrench ourselves away from a bond we experienced as bondage. We have broken away from a dependency on a parent, a friend or a lover, because the relationship was built on false gifts. Now we are free but alone. Having severed these links, we ask: "How do we form life-giving relationships? What if all human connections are bondage? What if all gifts end by enslaving us?" The good gift shows us another way. Because the generous giver lets go of the gift, we are released from demands for compensation and restitution. We are free but still bound in gratitude. Yet this is a bond of delight rather than constraint.

Gratitude bonds us to the gift and to its giver—a parent or friend or God. The goal of gratitude is not fully to repay the debt, since this is impossible. What would be an appropriate price to pay for the gift of our life? How would we determine the fair-market rate for our good health or the going price of an abiding friendship? Gratitude instead awakens us to the graciousness of the giver and prepares us to be generous ourselves. We are inducted into the community of gift givers, an assembly of passionate and responsible adults whose lives witness to the truth that, as Meister Eckhart puts it, "the fruitfulness of a gift is the only gratitude for the gift."

The Defeat of Gratitude

Gratitude is constantly under threat, undermined by cultural forces that argue for a different response. In a consumer society those accustomed to abundance easily fall into a sense of entitlement. With privileged lives we develop a demanding posture toward the world. "I deserve all that I have, and I expect this abundance to continue." Suspicion and ingratitude accompany our insistence that society not fail our ever-expanding expectations.

If entitlement arises in abundance, resentment grows in settings of scarcity. Aware that many of society's valued resources are not available to them, deprived people slide easily toward indignation. "Where are the goods this society has promised to all? Why is my family, and those like us, constantly denied our share?" Resentment can sometimes be forged into the resilient strength of resistance, a foundation for social change. But both entitlement and resentment keep the heart focused on present lack or fear of future loss, unmindful of the everyday blessings of life.

A particularly American lust for independence contributes to the defeat of gratitude. In this culture we have learned to associate dependence with weakness. We are urged to stand on our own two feet, we are warned not to be beholden to anyone, we are reminded that we only get what we pay for. Influenced by this pervasive cultural attitude, any experience of personal dependence feels like constraint, or even a belittling of our adult autonomy.

This cultural suspicion is reinforced for some of us by painful personal history, teaching us that gifts usually arrive with strings attached. Perhaps we can remember times when emotional support became manipulative, when caring actions deteriorated into constraint. Some gifts do indeed bind us in a demeaning indebtedness. Others entrap us in a dependency meant to diminish us. Here what is given comes not from generosity but out of a desire to control.

Being grateful moves us to do more than give thanks; we are eager to hand on the gift we have received. Gratitude lifts us out of ourselves. Being grateful locates us where we belong, on the shared journey of generosity that moves from the previous generation to the next. We recognize that we dwell in a community of gift giving. We can experience a new intimacy with both our benefactors and our beneficiaries.

The Dynamic of Generosity

The gifts you have received you should also give as gifts.

—MATTHEW 10:8

A community of gift givers is a gathering place for the generous. A group that lives under contract must be concerned about rules of exchange and the binding structures of constraint. A generous community lives by covenant, the free and responsible bestowal of gifts. The world of contracts teaches us the important lessons of duty and obligation. But in the world of covenant we learn to trace the connections between gratitude and generosity.

The interdependence of a vital community reminds us that we are not the owners of our abilities or our ideals. Our hold on these aspects of life is more mysterious than possession and control. We are stewards of resources received, not exclusive owners. True gifts cannot become simply private possessions. Feelings of gratitude remind us that, in Hyde's words, "our gifts are not fully ours until they have been given away." This insight is the heart of generosity.

Mentoring is one expression of generosity across the generations, especially relevant in the senior years. By this point in life many adults have been successful in roles of adult responsibility. As parents and teachers, as skilled workers and business leaders, as professionals and politicians they have developed competence and exercised power over several decades. Moving through mid-life toward their sixties and seventies, many adults recognize a generational shift. Younger people, many of whom we have trained and whose careers we have championed, are now eager for greater responsibility. As long as we occupy the places of leadership, little room is open for this younger cohort. The invitation to let go arises—sometimes from outside demands, but often from inner voices as well. At first we are likely to resist; surely it is too early. Almost by definition the next generation is not ready yet! But soon maturity and circumstance prevail. Even if with some regret, we embrace the asceticism of separation. In generosity and hope we cast our lot with the future.

For Christians, Jesus' departure from his beloved community offers the paradigm of this act of generosity. In his powerful presence, his trusted companions were content to forever remain disciples, dependent on his forceful personality. In his sudden absence—traumatic though it was—they were drawn into the leadership vacuum. Now, decisions about how the group would proceed were theirs to make. Jesus' absence was filled in part by the coming of the Spirit on Pentecost and in part by their own embrace of the mission before them. The disciples, deprived of Jesus' physical presence, became leaders. Removing himself from the community was Jesus' act of *generous absence*.

"The labor of gratitude is generosity." Gifted, we learn to give gifts; grateful, we grow generous. And generosity's final gift is letting go—of friends who have to leave and of children who must grow up. The gift must keep on giving. We cannot package it or protect it from the future. If we are fully blessed, we come to accept this mystery. Even as we let go of our own life we are grateful. The final word is thanks.

Forgiveness—Gratitude and Generosity

Forgiveness . . . is the hope of our humanity, since it wields the power to break the cycles of violence.

—MARJORIE HEWITT SUCHOCKI

Forgiveness is perhaps generosity's finest act. Forgiving those who have offended us does not come easily. We may choose to hold this offense over their heads, to harbor the resentment as we savor our wounds. There is bitter profit to be made here. And yet we may also choose to forgive, generously seeking to heal the bonds between us that have been broken. Forgiveness, of course, is not always ours to offer; this healing action is sometimes a gift we must wait to receive. And when we are forgiven, gratitude floods our heart.

Forgiveness is an evolved capacity allowing us to abandon our right to vengeance and to surrender our claim over those who offended us. Releasing the debt that an offender has incurred opens the future to a different kind of relationship. By changing the past, forgiveness opens the possibility of a new future.

Over many centuries retribution and vengeance were defended as human rights. This age-old commitment to paying *in kind* for an offense received leaves a toxic residue that infects future generations— what Paul Ricoeur calls *diseased memories* and *hereditary hatreds*. The refusal of forgiveness, he adds, "perpetuates a culture of contempt." Ricoeur muses poetically on the sudden advent in human history of this remarkable capacity to forgive. After millennia of vengeance and violent retribution "we hear a voice announcing, 'there is forgiveness.' This voice is silent, but it is not mute. Silent, because there is no clamor of what rages; not mute because not deprived of speech." Ricoeur concludes by linking forgiveness with humanity's richest resources. "There is forgiveness as there is joy, as there is wisdom, extravagance, love." He concludes: "Love, indeed. Forgiveness belongs to the same family."

George Vaillant defines forgiveness as "a willingness to abandon one's right to resentment, negative judgment and indifferent behavior towards one who unjustly injured us, while fostering the undeserved qualities of compassion, generosity and even love toward him or her." Marjorie Hewitt Suchocki affirms that "forgiveness holds the possibility of breaking the chain of violence."

Forgiveness is not a quick fix. Suchocki links forgiveness with a transformation of memory, empathy and imagination. This generous action demands an accurate memory of past offenses, empathy for others in the present and an imaginative vision of how things could be otherwise. And forgiveness requires a profound transformation of emotions—anger, bitterness and the desire for revenge. How does this transformation take place? What is the grace of forgiveness?

Forgiveness begins in the transformation of memory—the hold the offense has on our past, binding us in emotions of bitterness and revenge. Grace appears in the invitation to let go of these souvenirs of wrongdoing. "Transformative memory is that remembrance of the past as past, opening one to a new moment."

The transformation of empathy allows us to see the present—and the offender—in a new light: this person is more than an offender. "Under the sign of forgiveness, the guilty person is to be considered capable of something other than his offenses and his faults." This invites a new judgment about the other: "You are better than what you have done." Here we are invited to let go of the moral high ground of the abused victim.

We can transform the future through imagining it as different—no longer bound by the age-old rules of vengeance. Embracing an alternate vision defends us against a future that remains flooded with anger. These transformations ground the self-transcendence of the one who forgives. In giving up our right to harbor vengeance, we leave an embittered self behind and move into a richer realm of human life. The one who forgives no longer stands morally superior to the forgiven; now both inhabit the world of vulnerable mortals, in which all are called both to offer and to seek forgiveness.

This self-transcendence liberates us. Our past is transformed from a place of harbored vengeance; our present is freed of bitter rumination about the offender; our future is liberated as a space replete with new possibilities, relieved of the demand for hatred and revenge.

13

The Works of
Justice and Mercy

*What does the Lord require of you but to do
justice, and to love mercy, and to walk humbly
with your God?*

—MICAH 6:8

The human penchant for violence is well established; we seldom
need reminders of its devastating effects. When *might is right* rules
the land and revenge serves as a channel of retribution, mercy rarely
comes into play. As true justice asserts its rightful claims, social life
becomes more secure. When mercy accompanies justice, full humanity flourishes.

Psychologists today discuss justice and mercy as evolved moral capacities. Across history, heroes and sages and saints have demonstrated
these exceptional qualities. But incorporating these strengths into the
structures of society has been a slow business. This gradual evolution
of justice is evident in the Bible itself. An early formulation appears in
the often-quoted indictment "an eye for an eye, a tooth for a tooth"
(Ex 21:23). The abiding appeal of this maxim is apparent today, in
tribal vendetta and in justifications of capital punishment. The Gospel
of Matthew records Jesus' explicit rejection of vindictive justice: "You
have heard that it was said, 'an eye for an eye and a tooth for a tooth.'
But I say to you, do not resist an evildoer. But if anyone strikes you
on the right cheek, turn the other also . . . Give to everyone who begs
from you, and do not refuse anyone who wants to borrow from you"
(Mt 5:38–39, 42). This astonishing text begins by questioning a then-
dominant form of justice and ends with a call for a merciful response.
These revolutionary words of Jesus are often overlooked, even today,
by those who attempt to justify vengeance as a biblical call.

Justice as a Moral Emotion

*Even though you offer me your burnt offer-
ings and grain offerings I will not accept them
. . . But let justice roll down like water and
righteousness like an ever-flowing stream.*

—AMOS 5

A sense of justice embraces a broad constellation of feelings: outrage at the unfairness we see around us; anger toward those we judge
to be responsible for people's pain; compassion for those who are
suffering; an urgent desire to do something to correct the situation
at hand.

Psychologists often discuss justice as a character trait: a steady
disposition or ongoing commitment to respond actively in situations
where interpersonal fairness or social equity are at risk. We might
also speak of justice as a passion—in the sense that someone has a
passion for sports or a passion for cooking. By passion here we mean
an engaged concern, an easily activated sense of caring. The arousal
of justice often includes keen awareness of the problem at hand and
a determined attempt to overcome the unfairness involved.

In its mature expression the disposition of justice emerges from the
desire that people receive what is due to them. And what is due to
people—to all in the human community—is that their lives may go
well. The virtue of justice expands to include our willingness to support other people's well-being and a broadened commitment to human
flourishing throughout society. As theologian Terry Veling comments,
"Justice is the debt we owe to those who have been denied the well-
being of human flourishing. Wherever we find people who lack basic
social goods that are rooted in their very dignity as human persons,
then justice is owed."

Justice and Mercy in Social Transformation

The call to mercy resounds throughout the Hebrew bible and the
New Testament. The effort to include the biblical understandings of
mercy in the larger discussion of justice is a significant development
in ethical theory today. Connecting justice and mercy is sometimes
complicated for American Christians due to a particular understanding
of justice that prevails in our legal system. In Western social theory
the foundations of justice are equality and fairness. Democracy, for

example, requires that the benefits and burdens of society should be available to all citizens. Laws are enacted to promote and protect equal treatment. And justice demands that these laws be applied fairly, that is, without bias in the favor of some or prejudice against others. This interpretation of justice is a sophisticated social concept. But as many critics have pointed out, these commitments to equality do not guarantee equal outcomes—how things actually turn out in people's lives.

In classic understandings of justice the social contract is assumed to include people who are free, equal, and independent. To assume such equality, as Martha Nussbaum notes, "all advantages and hierarchies among human beings that are created by wealth, birth, class and so on are imagined away." The common status of *strict independence* implies, as Michael Sandel observes, a kind of moral individualism in which we are responsible only for what we have freely committed ourselves to. In this vision of individuality, "we can't make sense of a range of moral and political obligations that we commonly recognize, even prize. These include obligations of solidarity and loyalty, historic memory and religious faith—moral claims that arise from the communities and traditions that shape our identity." Sandel concludes: "Unless we think of ourselves as encumbered selves, open to moral claims we have not willed, it is difficult to make sense of these aspects of our moral and political experience."

In American cultural understanding, justice is based on fairness. People have a right to expect fair treatment. In our dealing with one another—and especially in the state's dealing with its citizens—everyone has a fair chance. This understanding is built on an appreciation of basic human rights, which are possessed by each person by reason of our common humanity. These rights function as universal principles that need to be promoted and protected. They are seen as inalienable; they cannot be taken away by any government body. In fact, a principal responsibility of a political state is to protect these individual rights so that they cannot be denied by any external force, not even by the government itself.

Justice rooted in human rights continues to be a significant goal throughout the world. This model functions as the framework for the Universal Declaration of Human Rights adopted by the General Assembly of the United Nations. In religious circles, too, this understanding of justice is rightly acknowledged as a major achievement of modern civilization. But the biblical vision goes further.

Theological ethics today both supports the gains and goals of this understanding of rights-based justice and tries to address and overcome its limitations. The biblical call to justice is about more than protecting privacy, more than holding everyone equally accountable to the same universal laws, more than simply ensuring that we stay out of one another's way. The biblical call to justice emerges from the recognition of human interconnections. Humans exist in community. Interrelatedness is an essential quality of our human experience.

Catholic moral tradition discusses the role of justice not simply as protecting and promoting individual rights but as supporting and safeguarding *right relationships*. Many contributors to social ethics today use this vocabulary, discussing justice in terms of recognizing, establishing and restoring relationships.

This focus on relationships still leaves the complex practical task of discerning our responsibility in any particular set of circumstances. This ethical discussion recognizes that different degrees of relatedness may carry different kinds of personal and social responsibility. But we begin with the recognition that as members of the human community we are already in relationship. From that starting point we attempt to work out the practical responsibilities we have toward one another.

True justice cannot be general; justice "lived out" must deal with particularity. So simply relying on universal laws is not sufficient. In fact, a general law established to serve all people sometimes turns out to hurt some groups, even if others benefit. General guidelines can set out a framework for discernment and decision-making. But just decisions, as moral decisions, must be worked out at the particular level. Only in terms of actual relationship can the claims of justice be determined and negotiated.

Seeing justice as essentially relational requires us to respect the relationships—personal, communal, civic, international—that arise in human connectedness. Recognizing justice as essentially relational opens us to the virtue of solidarity.

Justice and the Virtue of Solidarity

David Hollenbach, an influential Catholic moral theologian, has explored the moral disposition of justice in terms of the *common good*. The common good may be defined as "goods we hold as public and agree to pursue in common." This idea points to those advantages that are not a matter of personal possession or individual achievement, but belong to all the members of a *commonwealth*. Some social philosophers today question the very existence of a common good; for them, society is a battleground where different interest groups contend for scarce resources. Yet the Catholic Church continues to advocate a common good that includes "the sum total of those conditions of social living whereby men and women are enabled more fully and readily to achieve their well-being." Hollenbach draws on the statements of Pope John Paul II to trace the links between the common good and solidarity.

John Paul II identified solidarity as the contemporary expression of the virtue of justice. He defined *solidarity* as "a firm and persevering determination to commit oneself to the common good; that is to the good of all and of each individual."

This "firm and persevering determination" is rooted in our recognition of human interdependence. Justice recognizes the interconnected web of relationships that make up contemporary society. In this web each of us—individually and communally—influences and is influenced by relationships that extend far beyond our own immediate actions.

This appreciation of human interdependence expands our capacity for empathy, widening the boundaries of those included as "our kind." This movement of moral maturity is supported, as John Paul II noted, by "the recognition of one's neighbors as fundamentally equal because they are living images of God, redeemed by the blood of Jesus Christ and placed under the permanent activity of the Holy Spirit."

Hollenbach examines three expressions of solidarity that shape the virtue of justice today. The first is emotional solidarity—an affective response. Here our heart is engaged. We are moved by another's plight, motivated to respond. Emotional solidarity reinforces a sense of connectedness. We recognize that a bond exists here, not simply a mental link but an emotional connection. These feelings of engaged concern strengthen our personal commitment to act for change.

Intellectual solidarity is a second expression of justice as a moral emotion. Here our commitment to other persons goes so far that we take seriously their beliefs, their world view. We want to understand more about how they experience the world and the values that make their life meaningful.

Parker Palmer has called such knowledge a kind of love. Getting to know others, their values, their orientation in life expands our options for making a sensitive response. We can enter into discussion with them even as we recognize that genuine differences exist. Through this dialogue we come to a better understanding of their world and to a clearer grasp of actions that can affirm us both.

So intellectual solidarity offers a starting point for dialogue that may lead to mutual appreciation. Dialogue does not require that we will agree. But a commitment to dialogue expresses mutual respect. Even if we continue to differ on major questions of value and action, we are still able to keep open the channels of communication.

This dialogue often helps to clarify and expand our perspective. Even if we do not in the end accept the values that others champion, in a genuine dialogue we take them seriously enough to engage in conversation and debate. And we know that being understood by others supports our sense of personal dignity. Being understood by others opens us to compromise and reconciliation.

Practicing justice means making emotional connections and seeking intellectual engagement—and more. Solidarity moves beyond tolerance. Now we put ourselves actively on the others' side. Committed to common action, we stand together in response to the pain of the world. Social solidarity includes an effort to understand the complexity of the situation that needs remedy. Often the practical situations that arouse our sense of justice are not easily solved. If injustices could be easily remedied, most problems would have been resolved long before we arrived on the scene! So a prudent pause—for study, for coalition building, for prayer—helps ensure that our actions in fact contribute to the resolution of the problem. But finally the commitment of justice requires social solidarity, a willingness to take positive actions to resolve injustice and support systemic change.

With this new focus we recognize that justice and love cannot be separated. Love can lead us to actions that are not required by justice. But love is not antithetical to justice. True justice cannot exist without love; love and justice are made for each other. And *mercy* is the face of love most directly connected with justice.

The Religious Emotion of Mercy

In all conversions from suffering to hope, from sin to release, and from despair to faith, mercy is the effective element which offers a future and enables change. Only mercy can transform hearts of stone into hearts of flesh.

—HEATHER CHAPPELL

Biblical scholars note that the Hebrew term for mercy, *hesed*, includes a range of affections—compassion and fidelity, kindness and generosity. *Hesed* implies feelings of tenderness, an affective bond of loyalty and a readiness to help. Scripture suggests that after the work of creation, being merciful is what Yahweh does best. In creation, life begins; in mercy, life can begin again. Mercy supports the liberating movement from captivity toward freedom. The ancient Israelites were slaves in Egypt; today's most crippling forms of bondage are poverty, addiction and sin.

The Christian understanding of mercy is rooted in core passages in the New Testament. The parable of the Good Samaritan raises mercy to the level of obligation toward all who are in need. The story of the Prodigal Son surprises us with its unexpected gift of merciful forgiveness. Startling passages in the Gospel of Matthew— proclaiming Christ's presence among us in those who are hungry or thirsty or imprisoned—shatter the cautious limits of our own outreach in care.

Moral theologian James Keenan defines mercy as "the willingness to enter into the chaos of others so as to answer them in their need." Keenan sees acts of mercy as central in Catholic religious sensitivity. Catholic spirituality has emphasized the *corporal works of mercy*, practices rooted in biblical imperatives: feed the hungry, give drink to the thirsty, shelter the homeless, clothe the naked, care for the sick, visit those in prison, bury the dead. These efforts of practical outreach are to be complemented by the *spiritual works of mercy*: give good counsel, teach the ignorant, admonish sinners, console the afflicted, pardon injuries, bear offenses patiently, pray both for those living and those who have died. Keenan traces the long history of the practice of mercy that extends from the earliest monasteries' welcome of travelers, no matter how poor or ill, to contemporary organizations, such as Catholic Relief Services and St. Vincent de Paul Society. Throughout the centuries we see hostels, hospitals, pilgrimage centers and orphanages maintained under religious auspices, often serving as models for social services developed later under state sponsorship.

In Keenan's view mercy invites us to reexamine our view of justice, seeing it with new eyes. "Mercy does not temper justice as so many believe; rather, mercy prompts us to see that justice applies to all, especially those most frequently without justice, those abandoned to the chaos of the margins." More specifically, "mercy prompts justice to find the neglected, the persecuted, the oppressed and to bring them into the solidarity of humanity by assisting them in the pursuit of their rights."

The Grace of Mercy

*Yahweh is a God of tenderness and grace; slow
to anger and abounding in mercy [hesed] . . .
showing kindness [hesed] to the thousandth
generation.*

—EXODUS 34:6; 20:6

Justice is especially sensitive to discussions focusing on human
rights, since society has responsibility to protect the rights of all its
citizens. Mercy raises wider questions of responsibility, recognizing
that some members of our communities experience greater needs.
What responsibility—if any—does society bear in the face of its
citizens' differing needs? Mercy insists that this question become
a legitimate part of society's concern, even if its members do not
initially agree on the appropriate response.

If justice honors universal principles that can be applied to all,
mercy respects differing circumstances, personal history, individual
capacity. If justice relies on rational judgment, mercy involves
heartfelt reflection as much as deductive reasoning. Mercy is not
irrational or mindless, but its energy comes from the heart. Mercy
asks something of us. If we are to display mercy, we may have to
relent, surrendering harsh judgments and releasing others from the
bonds of indebtedness.

In the biblical tradition, as Terry Veling points out, mercy is often
a surprise blessing, a movement of mildness or moderation where we
might have expected harshness. Mercy is manifest in the response
of unexpected leniency or the choice to refrain from inflicting pain.
The surprise of mercy reflects the graciousness of God's favor and
care for us.

Justice, bound by its own legal limits, cannot bring about the
full well-being to which it aspires. As Veling notes, "Underlying all
quests for justice stands the whole gravity of love." He identifies the
politics of mercy: "Such a politics diverges from strictness toward
forbearance, from cruelty toward 'a slow, gentle fostering of what
good there may be.'" He concludes, "A politics of mercy recognizes
that 'the human world is held together by pity and fellow-feeling.'"
Mercy transports us beyond the narrow confines of justice and
righteousness. "Go and learn what this means: 'I desire mercy, not
sacrifice.' For I have come to call not the righteous but sinners" (Mt
9:13). To be sure, mercy is good news for justice.

Mercy evokes compassion. This profound emotion moves beyond the coolly rational call of duty toward a deeper connection with those who suffer. In compassion, we recognize that these sometimes strangers, too, are "like us"—possessing an essential dignity, worthy to share in the goods of the world, themselves potential contributors to the well-being of us all.

Mercy plays an important role, too, in forgiving our enemies. Here we face those who have injured us, those whom our own moral calculus finds blameworthy, those we judge to be at fault and unrepentant. Mercy's goal is not to deny moral fault or excuse the evil done. What mercy offers instead is a softened heart.

Mercy is not yet forgiveness, but its compassion is often the precursor of our genuine efforts toward reconciliation. Compassion comes in the visceral recognition that the wrong-acting person—this individual responsible for genuine harm—is *more than* these evil acts and intentions. In spite of blameworthy actions and well-deserved guilt, the injurer is, like each of us, a vulnerable human being still worthy of respect. While mercy does not deny the call to justice, its softened heart undermines hatred and vindictiveness. Through the power of compassion we can be moved to recognize the plight of our enemies and actively to desire the well-being even of those who have harmed us.

The Truth and Reconciliation Commission that was part of the movement toward social reconciliation in post-apartheid South Africa offers a vivid example of the wider social framework of mercy. Under the leadership of Nelson Mandela, Desmond Tutu and others, a series of formal public sessions was scheduled. These were neither legal proceedings nor judicial hearings. Instead, offenders on both sides of this national struggle—apartheid supporters and resistance fighters—were offered legal amnesty in exchange for public testimony acknowledging their responsibility for violent actions. In the presence of these perpetrators, victims were encouraged and supported in this difficult effort to offer personal accounts of the pain and humiliation they had experienced. And perpetrators could speak about what they had done and their feelings about their actions. The goal was a truthful account of the suffering inflicted and endured, leading not to legal recrimination but to social healing.

Paul Gilbert describes this process as *restorative justice:* "The emphasis is far less on making the perpetrator suffer and more on trying to create healing and change in both perpetrator and victim. They are brought together and directly confronted with the pain of the other. The focus is on mutual empathy: in the perpetrator a sense of remorse, sadness and guilt; in the victim, movement toward forgiveness and acceptance."

Mercy is a cultivated grace. We often experience its arousal as a gift more than as a direct result of a personal decision. But we can dispose ourselves to this heartfelt response. Through these formative and transformative practices of solidarity and prayer, we strengthen this basic human capacity so that mercy, too, becomes a reliable character strength.

14

Emotions
in Spiritual Transformation

*It is characteristic of the good spirit to give cour-
age and strength, consolation, tears, inspiration,
and peace, making things easy and removing
all obstacles, so that the soul may make further
progress in good works.*

—Ignatius Loyola

At the end of the fourth century two of the greatest theologians of
early Christianity—Gregory of Nyssa and Augustine of Hippo—offered strikingly different interpretations of the role of emotions in the
life of faith. Augustine, in his *Confessions*, saw grief as a self-indulgent
weakness and a source of shame. For Gregory, this disruptive passion
served the therapeutic purpose of turning our broken hearts toward
God.

Gregory: Emotions in God's Pedagogy

Gregory, like other spiritual writers of his time, struggled to understand the place of passion in Christian life. At his brother's death
Gregory was troubled by his tears, which he saw as a stark reminder
of his own mortality. His sister Macrina cautioned him not to deny
his deep sadness: "We would not know how little we understand the
soul if we did not give way to the full instinctive weight of grief." The
passion of grief surely disturbs us but need not be a source of shame.
Instead, we should open ourselves to its deeper significance. Benefiting
from Macrina's good counsel, Gregory became convinced of the moral
quality of the emotions. For Gregory, "fear engenders obedience, anger

courage, cowardice caution; the desiring faculty fosters in us divine and pure pleasures."

Emotions—even those that provoke pain and disrupt tranquility— are part of what Gregory calls *a divine pedagogy*. "The emotions can themselves be redeemed and even play an essential role in our salvation." Gregory insists that scripture gives evidence of passion's positive role: the Book of Proverbs proclaims fear as the source of wisdom. Paul acknowledges the *godly grief* that leads to repentance and salvation, in contrast to *worldly grief,* which yields only death (2 Cor 7:10). The passions are not oriented to evil but are, in fact, "essential for the soul's ascent to and union with God in the present life."

Gregory's optimism included the conviction that creation's beauty leads us to the Source of all beauty. "Hope always draws the soul from the beauty which is seen to what is beyond, always kindles the desire for the hidden through what is constantly perceived." In its first instance desire is a divinely bestowed force within us. Our desire echoes the Creator's desire for our very existence. For Gregory, in the words of scholar Melvin Laird, desire is our "homing instinct for God."

Gregory writes that spiritual growth is marked by a gradual transformation as we progress over a lifetime toward our Creator. Reflecting a dominant image of the Eastern Church, Gregory understood that all humans are being gathered up into their Creator in a process of *divinization* or *deification.* At the close of his commentary on the Song of Songs, Gregory offers a breathtaking vision of the goal of this transformation of humankind: "Every evil will be destroyed. God will be all in all, and all persons will be united together in fellowship of the Good, Christ Jesus our Lord, to whom be glory and power forever and ever. Amen." Such a radical optimism would be unthinkable to Augustine and, as a result of Augustine's pervasive influence, to much of Western Christianity.

Augustine: Spiritual Danger of Powerful Emotion

Augustine's personal experience with passion led him to different conclusions concerning emotions and conversion. Convinced that human nature was essentially damaged in the original sin of Adam and Eve, he judged that our natural inclinations could no longer be trusted to guide us on the spiritual journey. All human senses had been rendered unreliable; the impulses and yearnings of the human spirit were likely to lead away from God and toward an idolatrous clinging to creatures. Hunger, curiosity and laughter were included in the list of movements of the heart that were no longer trustworthy. Self-deception was now humanity's default position.

Augustine's vision of conversion is profoundly different from Gregory's. Drawing again on personal experience, he insists that whole-hearted conversion to God demands a radical break. Full response to God's love requires a rejection of one's former ways; the past is to be set aside in favor of a new spiritual identity. Central to Augustine's vision is an antagonism in which the sacred rejects the secular and the "city of God" stands superior to and distant from the "city of man."

This dramatic conversion experience—involving a profound shift away from one's previous life—was familiar to St. Paul, as well as to Martin Luther. In much of subsequent Christian spirituality these wrenching life-changing experiences offered heroic images of spiritual transformation. The more ordinary graces of Christian life, which marked the transforming journeys of Gregory and countless others, would receive less attention.

For Augustine, life is a pilgrimage through a land of broken promises and the mirage of earthly delights. Restlessness marked his spiritual journey, driven by refusal to accept anything less than the divine object of his heart's desire. Augustine's intellectual and moral influence on Western Christianity has been profound. Resonating with his conviction that "all things are passing away," devout Christians have sometimes turned away from both enjoyment of the world's pleasures and active involvement in the struggle for social justice and political reform.

A Contemporary View:
The Role of Emotions in Conversion and Transformation

Psychologist Peter Hill traces emotions, negative and positive, as essential companions in spiritual transformation. He begins by recalling the classic contributions of psychologist and philosopher William James. In *The Varieties of Religious Experience* James's intent is to examine the psychological underpinnings of personal faith commitments and the experience of spirituality.

James describes the journey of spiritual transformation as the movement from the *ego-self* to a *sacred identity*. This movement involves the shaping or reshaping of the "habitual center of personal energy." James includes in this psychological core "the cluster of ideas and values to which a person is practically committed and from which the person acts meaningfully in the world." For James, religious symbols and spiritual ideals function as part of this psychological core, providing a larger belief structure that helps people define the kind of person they want to be and the kind of life they desire to live.

Working within the secular milieu at the beginning of the twentieth century in the United States, James was determined to offer a philosophical justification for religious faith, and for the centrality of religion in the meaning system of many people. He was not advocating a particular religious creed. But in his judgment what is unique about the embrace of religious faith—as distinguished from other world views that people use to ground their sense of personal meaning—is its potential for transforming influence in the lives of people who embrace it.

Religious faith, of course, does not carry such positive potential for all people. In some lives religious beliefs become a source of pathology. Bigotry, for example, often proceeds under the banner of religious belief. Beyond this intolerant fringe, a large proportion of people performs religious duties primarily to fulfill social expectations. Here religious practice becomes simply part of a well-established routine, what James called a "dull habit" rather than a "hot center of concern." Yet for many people spiritual sensitivity expands consciousness and enhances life. For them, religious faith serves as a source and support for personal transformation.

James studied classic written accounts describing the personal experience of profound religious conversion. From that analysis he concluded that when religious faith is transformative in people's lives, much more than cognitive belief is involved. The intellectual content of religious truths is not insignificant, to be sure. But at the core of the conversion experience are powerful emotions, leading to a "newly discovered state of assurance." Thus faith involves emotional response as well as cognitive engagement.

Hill expands James's analysis of the ways in which emotions are involved in spiritual growth. He takes up the two movements that James discusses: *conversion,* the initial and often wrenching turning away from sin; and *transformation,* the deepening process of spiritual maturity that has been identified in the reform Christian traditions as striving for righteousness and in the Catholic tradition as the pursuit of holiness. Emotions play a significant role in both these movements. Hill suggests that an initial religious conversion is often provoked—or at least accompanied—by painful feelings. In classical Christian spirituality this has been known as the *purgative way,* during which unhealthy habits, self-absorbed behavior, and sinful actions are confronted and purged from one's life. The subsequent *transformative journey*, as one moves through and beyond the regret-filled conversion, is motivated and accompanied by more positive emotions.

Hill sets out his model of conversion in terms of four *crises* of meaning and purpose. Hill's model of transformation is also shaped by four factors, which he names *affirmations*.

Crises and Conversion

A negative mood of dissatisfaction often marks early stages of a religious conversion. Discomfort with our present life triggers a desire to abandon what no longer satisfies in the hope of finding a richer, deeper way to live. Four interrelated crises are likely to be part of the process of conversion.

A crisis of purpose. One of life's major motivations is striving for goals. We long to know that our life is oriented toward some significant task, some better state of affairs. But at various points in life we may have to confront the painful question: Is this all there is? Early goals and once-cherished values have turned to ashes; they did not keep the promises we thought they were making to us. Feelings of confusion, disorientation and disappointment take possession of us. Anxiety increases as we struggle to find a more meaningful direction in life.

A crisis of personal morality. For some people the crisis that triggers spiritual conversion touches on morality. We acknowledge that we have fallen short of a personal standard of behavior or that our previous moral standards are themselves not adequate to the complexities of life. These earlier rules do not support the role that we want to play in the human community or the range of our responsibility for ourselves and others. We may judge that we have fallen short of a particular moral code. With feelings of guilt, shame and even self-loathing, we long for a new way of life. This crisis may generate energy to turn away from this destructive behavior and turn toward new sources of moral meaning and motivation.

A crisis of efficacy. Here painful emotions arise as we recognize personal inadequacy. Experiences of failure and disappointment lead us to confront the reality of our own deficiency. We become more aware of physical limitations, intellectual inadequacy or social disadvantages. Emotions of fear or frustration, or even a sense of impotence, arise. These painful feelings may move us to reconsider what life means and to search for the religious symbols and belief system to reconnect us with a sense of value and contribution.

A crisis of self-worth. Despair threatens as we become aware that we have fallen short of our own expectations, that we have lost some vital connection with our own best self. Negative self-judgments and a sense of self-doubt arise, often accompanied by envy of others who seem more securely rooted in a sense of self-worth. A painful sense of hopelessness may devastate us; we feel worthless. This negative mood invites us to look for some larger source of worth.

Through these crises, the "hot spot" of our own consciousness becomes more open to a religious frame of meaning. For James, this is the psychological basis of conversion. And as the spiritual journey continues, he suggests, new dynamics come into play. The tumultuous period of dissatisfaction and regret gives way to the more positive movements of spiritual transformation. Hill now expands James's discussion by focusing on the insights and emotions awakened on the journey of continuing spiritual growth.

Spiritual Transformation: Four Affirmations

As religious consciousness matures through initial conversion toward ongoing transformation, new patterns of discipleship emerge. Positive emotions often motivate and accompany this stage of the journey. Hill describes this shift in terms of four affirmations.

An affirmation of ultimacy. For some, this affirmation begins in experiences of wonder and awe, in a new appreciation of beauty marked by grateful acknowledgment of the Creator. Others are moved by expressions of forgiveness and reconciliation, or by witnessing other people's courageous or compassionate actions. For still others, this affirmation leads to the acceptance of Jesus as one's personal savior. In each of these shifts we notice an expanding spiritual consciousness and a new, if tentative, assurance of transcendence in one's life. These emotions reinforce a sense of wholeness and renewal; ultimately, reality is on our side. Characteristic emotions here are contentment, appreciation, serenity, joy—aspects of what we might call spiritual consolation.

An affirmation of value. Spiritual transformation includes a more positive reappraisal of our life and reframes a sense of personal purpose. We realize there are values in life worth living for—and perhaps even values worth dying for. We acknowledge a value framework wider than getting our own way. This does not demand denouncing our needs. But personal goals are now situated in a much larger appraisal of life's purpose and significance. This affirmation is, as we might expect, accompanied by a new sense of humility, a recognition that we are only a small part of the drama of life. We may also experience a movement of thanksgiving, gratitude that we are in contact with this deeper dimension of value. And we embrace the emotion of joy as we align our life with this larger perspective of meaning and purpose.

An affirmation of empowerment. Here we experience the paradox of power. Acknowledging the limits of our own resources, we recognize God's power surrounding and supporting us. Paul described this mysterious dynamic: "It is no longer I who live, but it is Christ who lives in me" (Gal 2:20). Letting go our usual self-absorption results in an expansion of self-confidence, a deeper sense of authenticity out of which our power comes. Or a new kind of self-control becomes significant, *ascetical* but not in the more traditional sense of self-denial or self-diminishment. Many people report a new movement of generosity and, in psychological terms, *generativity*. They recognize—again paradoxically—that their power, limited though it is, is strong enough for the duties and desires that now guide their life. Now they can risk spending themselves, using their resources in support of people and purposes that go beyond narrow self-interest.

An affirmation of self-worth. Rid of the illusion we once held about our independent power, we come to see that our value rests on a stronger foundation. This affirmation does not deny our talents and energy and convictions. Our gifts are real, but ultimately they arise from a Source beyond ourselves. With this comes a deeper appreciation of personal dignity and self-confidence. Here a new sense of humility is joined by the emotion of healthy pride.

The larger point for both William James and Peter Hill is the recognition that religious conversion and the journey toward holiness are not a matter of will power or rational decisions alone but entail a range of emotional experience. Guilt and fear should not dominate this journey, but they may be expected to appear at key intervals. Warm feelings and seasons of joy are not guaranteed companions in religious living, though we may confidently expect these blessings at various stages of the passage. A richer appreciation of the dynamics of the positive emotions—broadening and building our psychological resources—may assist our movement along the mysterious journey of spiritual transformation.

Consolation and Desolation

In the *Spiritual Exercises* Ignatius of Loyola wisely cautions the person moving through the painful passage of conversion to be alert to the alternating movement of joy and sadness. Writing in the sixteenth century, he discusses this rhythm in the idiom of good and bad spirits. A person following the path of virtue characteristically experiences the positive mood Ignatius identifies as consolation. "It is characteristic of the good spirit to give courage and strength, consolation, tears, inspiration, and peace, making things easy and removing all obstacles, so that the soul may make further progress in good works." For Ignatius, consolation was both a gift of God and a signal that one is progressing on the spiritual journey. Consolation names "any interior joy that calls and attracts to heavenly things." This mood provides solace and comfort, reinforcing that we are on the right path.

But this fragile mood is easily dislodged as our mind and heart turn to less wholesome thoughts and desires. Then a debilitating mood is likely to invade the soul. "I call desolation . . . darkness of the soul, turmoil of the mind, inclination to low and earthly things, restlessness resulting from many disturbances." This foul mood takes other forms as well: "It is also desolation when a soul finds itself completely apathetic, tepid, sad, and separated as it were, from its Creator and Lord." Ignatius sees in this distress the work of the evil spirit. "It is common for the evil spirit to cause anxiety and sadness, and to create obstacles based on false reasoning, through preventing the soul from making further progress."

Desolation depletes our energy and drains away joy. Depression and desolation are sometimes confused, since both seem to occupy the same place in our soul. Experienced spiritual guides offer this distinction: *depression* accurately describes the state of a defeated psyche, often closely related to hormonal and other neurochemical imbalances; *desolation* names a deflated spirit. In Ignatius's understanding, this distress alerts us that we may be veering away from the path. This unhappy mood—painful as it is—may function as a gift, alerting us that we are losing our way.

Consolation as a Cultivated Mood

> [Consolation] is a faith-based experience, a sense
> of expanding in harmony with what is deepest
> in us, the Spirit in us.
> —MICHAEL PAUL GALLAGHER, SJ

Michael Paul Gallagher reflects on the Ignatian vision of consolation as an interior mood of abiding joy and also a cultivated attitude that grounds a balanced orientation toward one's life in the world.

For Gallagher, "In large options and small reactions, consolation is an experience of being-in-tune-with-Christ."

The positive mood of consolation steadies us in the face of the disheartening experiences of daily life that threaten to overwhelm our spirit. "Without such a starting point in consolation, one is in danger of rejecting entire ways of life as utterly beyond the reach of the gospels." Cultivating a mood of consolation does not require overlooking the sobering reality of the world's distress. "The call to ground oneself in a certain consolation does not close the door to prophetic denunciation of what may be dehumanizing. Paradoxically we need to be able to see the desolation induced by the culture while guarding consolation as the ground of our Christian response."

In the Ignatian vision, consolation is a determining factor in the practice of spiritual decision-making or *discernment*. Discernment allows us to read a social situation in a distinctly Christian fashion. It allows us to see the workings of the Spirit in our own times. In a mood of consolation we still recognize a culture's illusions and temptations, but we are also able to see there the "signs of hope and real hunger, fruits of the spirit."

If we surrender to a mood of desolation, "a fairly fruitless tone of blanket moaning about reality will take over." In an abiding mood of consolation—as much gift as achievement—we will be more able to criticize unhealthy dynamics in a culture while retaining "a trust that these shadows are not the whole story: consolation means acknowledging that there are also authentic values within the culture which need liberating from the deceptions."

Emotions shape our lives even as we craft disciplines and strategies for managing our feelings. Moods of consolation and desolation sometimes descend on us without any apparent reason. But we are not impotent here. By developing practices of paying attention and giving thanks, by fasting from distractions that dissipate us, we befriend our emotional world. In these exercises—these spiritual practices—we are often blessed by movements of confidence and hope. These abiding feelings register in us as consolation.

15

Religion and Ways of Knowing

For now we see in a mirror, dimly, but then we will see face to face. Now I know only in part; but then I will know fully.

—1 CORINTHIANS 13:12

Religion embraces dimensions of human experience that stretch beyond the obvious and the evident. The great religious traditions of the world—East and West—testify that there is more to life than we can measure or count. Adam Phillips remarks, "Religion has historically been the language for people to talk about the things that mattered most to them." He adds, "The things we value most—the gods and God, love and sexuality, mourning and amusement, character and inspiration, the past and the future—are neither measurable or predictable."

Writing to the early Christian community, Paul turned to poetic imagery to describe our clouded vision of life's meaning and purpose. "For now we see in a mirror, dimly, but then we will see face to face. Now I know only in part; but then I will know fully" (1 Cor 13:12). In this passage Paul used the Greek word *enigma* to point to the puzzlement that constantly confronts humans. Paul predicts that we can catch a glimpse of deeper truths, though our perception will be indirect (as in a reflection) and often muddled (as in a clouded mirror).

Scholars in many disciplines today are attempting to understand the distinctive kinds of awareness that move us beyond the visible and the obvious. Richard Shweder includes in this domain "those inspirations (of religion, of tradition, of individual literary or scientific genius) that take us beyond our senses to real places where even logic cannot go." Throughout this book we have explored the ways that healing emotions open the mind and heart to deeper experience. Absorbed in

147

wonder or staggered by an awesome experience, we are more than simply receptive. In this vulnerable state we are actively engaged, struggling to come to terms with what we cannot comprehend. The bounds of our comprehension and certitude are stretched. Religious awareness is often the fruit of this expanding consciousness.

With the rehabilitation of emotion we confirm both the breadth and limitations of human knowing. As emotions and intuitions are recognized as carriers of authentic insight, our appreciation of the world widens, prying open space for religious inspiration and insight.

We Know So Little— The Limits of Our Knowing

Mathematical models and controlled experimentation have dramatically enhanced our understanding of the natural world. But, as John Cottingham recognizes, "there are swathes of human life where understanding and enrichment do not come through the methods of science; these include not just poetry, music, novels, theatre, and all the arts, but the entire domain of human emotions and human relationships." Scientific reasoning is but one facet of human intelligence. For these other dimensions—intuition, inspiration, insight—we lack the words that would give them a comparable status. Cottingham concludes: "It would be outrageous arrogance to suppose that the limits of our puny human scientific or even conceptual resources must necessarily determine the actual limits of reality."

Susan Neiman comments on our ambiguous situation: "We know, in general, quite a lot. We know that our capacities for error are great, and our capacities for self-deception even greater. We know that our motives are usually mixed . . . We also know that we are free." She concludes, "Given all that we know, humility about what we don't know is a moral imperative."

A century ago William James explored the kind of knowing that is part of religious experience. In a wide-ranging discussion he drew attention to the curious consciousness we experience at the margin of our awareness. Driving an automobile or riding a bicycle, we focus our attention on the road ahead. But at the same time we are aware of activity at the edge of the path, at the "fringe" of our direct concentration. If another vehicle suddenly approaches from a side road, we are able to respond defensively, having glimpsed its approach at the periphery of our vision.

The fringe marks a threshold of consciousness, suggesting there is more to be known. James reminds us, "Our normal waking consciousness is but one special type of consciousness, while all about it, apart from it by the flimsiest of screens, there lie potential forms of consciousness entirely different." At any one time we can grasp only a narrow slice of a reality that vastly exceeds our comprehension. The image of the fringe suggests that we would benefit from paying more attention to the periphery of our awareness, appreciating the *vague* intimations and insights that arise in the realms of art and religion.

We Know So Much— The Intelligence of the Unconscious

Two paradoxical aspects of human knowledge are widely supported by current research. We know much less about reality than we once thought, but we actually know more than we are usually conscious of. Research in the neurosciences is providing an exciting portrait of the complex human operation that produces intuitions, moral insights and passionate virtues.

Neuroscientist Gerd Gigerenzer writes, "We think of intelligence as a deliberate, conscious activity guided by the laws of logic. Yet much of our mental life is unconscious, based on processes alien to logic: gut feelings, or intuitions." He reminds us that intelligence is not identical with conscious thought. The paradox is that "the cerebral cortex in which the flame of consciousness resides is packed with unconscious processes, as are the older parts of our brain." He adds, "The unconscious parts of our minds can decide without us—the conscious self—knowing its reasons." This is the case, for example, in the regulation of our breathing and in the release of hormones that energize us to act in the face of danger. These vital functions are activated within the autonomic nervous system, the network of neural pathways that generate energy to support our most basic physical activities—stimulating digestion, fight or flight behaviors, moving the body through space.

David Myers expands on this idea: "Our minds process vast amounts of information outside of consciousness, beyond language." In fact, "most of our everyday thinking, feeling and acting operate outside conscious awareness." We are aware of many things (the pressure of our feet on the floor, the temperature in the room) without being consciously attuned to this information. "More than we realized over a decade ago, thinking occurs not on stage, but off stage, out of sight." This realization leads Myers to a significant conclusion: "The growing scientific appreciation of non-rational, intuitive forms of knowing lends credence to spirituality."

How We Know—
Intuition and the Wisdom of the Body

As the unconscious workings of the brain cross the border into consciousness, we enter the realm of intuition. Psychologists and neuroscientists today are demystifying this movement. Neural connections throughout our body—in our muscles, gut, lungs—send signals to the spinal cord and on to the brain. These arousals, part of the wisdom of the body, offer alerts and cautions about our physical well-being. This neural activity also supports intuition. Daniel Siegel describes the process: "Such input from the body forms a vital source of intuition and powerfully influences our reasoning and the way we create meaning in our lives."

Our five senses continuously flood the nervous system and brain with new information. Researchers now identify a "sixth sense"—the dynamic through which this amalgam of information, initially registered in muscles and nerves and hormonal flow, is accessed by the brain. This *wisdom of the body* remains largely out of consciousness but sometimes surfaces in the form of hunches or intuitions. A "seventh sense," which can be developed through practices of mindfulness, brings this inner state of mental and emotional activity into consciousness. All of these senses make us more present to our life, promoting our freedom to choose ways of acting that make for a richer, more meaningful existence.

Let's look at an ordinary example of intuition at work. A manager prepares to leave home for a day at the office. Exiting the front door, she starts walking toward her automobile but then stops. An awareness arises: "I was going to bring something with me this morning, but what?" At this point, she *knows* but does not know. After a brief pause, the realization comes: "Ah, yes! I promised I would bring that new novel with me today to loan to my colleague." Some intuitive signal, crossing into consciousness, brought her to a halt, then surfaced in awareness a moment later.

Gerd Gigerenzer defines intuitive knowledge as insight "that appears quickly in consciousness; whose underlying reasons we are not fully aware of, and [yet] is strong enough to act on." He adds: "Intuition is more than impulse and caprice; it has its own rationale."

The role of intuition as *gut feelings* has taken on new importance, as military researchers explore ways to improve soldiers' ability to detect imminent danger—a hidden explosive devise, an ambush nearby. Here a gut feeling "may arise before a person becomes conscious of what the brain has registered." A soldier becomes instinctually aware that something is out of place, the road surface is too smooth, the street scene too quiet. "As the brain tallies cues, big and small, consciously or not, it may send out an alarm before a person fully understands why."

Inspiration names another movement of intuition, in which insight is "made manifest." The word *inspiration* is rooted in the image of "breathing in" *(in-spire)*. Here knowledge is not actively sought or positively grasped but receptively embraced. Recognizing this element of receptivity, poetic accounts of inspiration often point to the role of spirits or muses or genii as sources of new awareness. Beyond poetry, the role of inspiration continues to be acknowledged as a source of artistic creativity and scientific discovery.

Haunting Awareness

Viewing an impressive painting we are made aware of a mood or emotion that somehow *inhabits* this picture. We cannot directly describe for ourselves or convincingly point out to someone else this intimation of meaning. Yet some compelling information has made its way, unbidden, into our consciousness. The artist has so arranged the light and shadow as to elicit a mood or emotion that we may say now *haunts* the portrait.

It is this quality of experience that art critic Peter Schjeldahl seeks to evoke in his description of the art of the Spanish painter El Greco: "The glory and the problem of El Greco is the same: spirituality . . . the awareness that glimmers at the head-spring of consciousness, prior to thought and feeling . . . as the primary fact of life, always on tap." Schjeldahl concludes, "Spiritual intimations trickle through all minds, however obscurely, and even while discounted or ignored." So it is with beautiful music. Beyond the tones that can be scientifically described, we become attentive to something more and something else—easy to experience yet difficult to name.

Modern sensibilities—with biases toward rationality and scientific objectivity—recoil at the image of *haunting*. The advances of the modern world seem to have permanently banished the ghosts that inhabited and inhibited so much of pre-modern life. And yet the ghosts will not disappear. Theater critic John Lahr of the *New Yorker* writes of the role of ghosts in dramas: "Can we agree that we're all haunted? The ghost world is part of our world. We carry within us the good and the bad, the spoken and unspoken imperatives of our missing loved ones . . . Conversations rarely stop at the grave. So when we encounter ghosts onstage, they both terrify and compel us; within their trapped energy is an echo of our own unresolved losses."

The Catholic Church, in its documents of the Second Vatican Council, sought to capture some of this haunting aspect of the mysterious presence of God. In a discussion of other religious traditions the council referred to "a certain perception of that hidden power which hovers over the course of things and over the events of human life." In a text focused on the church itself, the council urged Christians to be mindful of all those "who in shadows and images seek the unknown God."

The rehabilitation of emotion that we have traced in this volume invites us to be more open to the elusive emotional arousals that arise in daily experience. Often, significant information is being offered us in these movements. Befriending such ghosts may open us to more of the world's wonders as well as to the mysterious presence of God.

Moral Insight

The recognition that emotions have cognitive content—are more than mere hormonal surges—suggests a positive role of emotions in moral life. Steven Pinker emphasizes the moral intuitions—such as fairness, compassion and trust—as the foundations of "the new science of the moral sense." Dacher Keltner summarizes an appreciation of moral intuition emerging among psychologists. Embodied emotions like compassion, gratitude and wonder, he acknowledges, serve as "powerful moral guides. They are upheavals that propel us to protect the foundations of moral communities—concerns over fairness, obligations, virtue, kindness, and reciprocity. Our capacity for virtue and concern over right and wrong are wired into our bodies."

Philosophers, too, are exploring moral awareness as more than the product of disciplined reason. Increasing attention is given to the significance of moral intuitions, functioning outside conscious rationality, in constructing a responsible life. Charles Taylor insists that our moral convictions are rooted in a "pre-reflective, inchoate orientation to good." Before we begin the rational reflection through which our moral convictions are clarified, we are intuitively aware of certain actions—lying, cheating, unprovoked violence—as incompatible with the good life. The source of such convictions often lies below the threshold of our conscious reasoning. Philosophers have sometimes resisted using the term *instinct,* with its traditional reference to biologically rooted impulses. But Taylor and others today find the term's biological resonance to be appropriate; these moral instincts are part of our evolutionary endowment. Building on this inheritance our communities and cultures *cultivate* in us enduring convictions about good and evil. Thus these instincts are very much social in character.

Religious Ways of Knowing

Philosophers continually try to clarify these intuitions, sometimes called the "fugitive sources" of insight. Taylor insists that we are in contact with a reality that inhabits us at a deeper level than any cognitive description we might offer. Religious rituals of grieving and gratitude and reverence "are designed to work on the visceral or spiritual register of being, below direct intellectual control." These rituals seek to tap the wellsprings of religious sensitivity that lie below the threshold of everyday comprehension.

"For now we see in a mirror, dimly, but then we will see face to face." Paul's words capture an essential aspect of religious knowing. Paul Avis offers yet another description of the limits of religious intuition: "The knowledge it gives is not like a noonday sun but (as Locke used to say) like the light of a candle in a dark room, sufficient to see our way—to make the moral commitment of faith that we are called to exercise as persons in a moral universe." The insight we gain through these moral intuitions, he reminds us, "is heuristic, not definitive; it is fragmentary, not total."

George Steiner reminds us that many of our most important insights are, indeed, gifts and revelations. "That which comes to call on us will very often do so unbidden. Even when there is a readiness, as in the concert hall, in the museum, in the moment of chosen reading, the true entrance into us will not occur by an act of will." Such revelations suggest "needs we knew not of."

The most sophisticated exploration of religious knowing comes from French philosopher Jean-Luc Marion. As a phenomenologist, Marion focuses on the fusion of intuition and concept in acts of human cognition. *Intuition,* for Marion, indicates all the information streaming into us through our senses; *concept* names the organization of this information by the mind.

Marion is particularly interested in those situations when the intuitions flooding our consciousness overwhelm us, making it difficult for

us to bring all the information into focus. Marion names this experience "an excess of intuition." Falling in love is an obvious example of
this kind of experience. To some extent we know what is happening,
but our mind and heart are nonetheless overwhelmed. We cannot get
our mind around this experience. In describing the enigma of love,
Paul Ricoeur says it well: "Ultimately, when two beings embrace, they
don't know what they are doing, they don't know what they want,
they don't know what they are looking for, they don't know what
they are finding."

Marion offers a number of examples of this excess of intuition.
A historical event, such as a war, provides the human mind with an
overwhelming flow of information; this is an *excess of quantity*. Endless interpretations are possible, but there remains simply too much
data to fathom fully. One knows what is taking place but cannot make
sense of the whole event.

A second example is of an *excess of quality*. Looking at a great
painting, we are flooded with powerful but elusive emotions. There
is so much to feel and appreciate. We continue gazing at the portrait
because we cannot thoroughly, once and for all, appreciate this beauty.
We cannot take it all in. We cannot *finish* looking at it.

For a third example Marion points to our experience of our own
body. We are intimately and deeply conscious of our physical self, yet
there is always more about this embodied self that we do not fully
grasp. There is more information flooding our senses than the mind
can handle. We understand much about our body, yet it continues to
be an enigma.

Marion is especially interested in how religious insight—information or intuitions that might reveal sources that transcend the obvious and the ordinary—is actually experienced. If God, whose reality
transcends our ordinary experience, does exist, we will encounter
this mystery only as an excess of intuition. Our consciousness would
be flooded with clues and hints without our being able to fully grasp
what is taking place. In his vocabulary the term *saturated phenomena*
describes experiences that are so overflowing—saturated—with intuition that our finite minds cannot begin to fathom their significance.

A chief characteristic of such awareness—of God's presence or
revelation—would not be scarcity (the lack of clear information),
but superabundance. The intuitions we undergo would be dazzling
and stupefying. The problem confronting us would not be lack of
light (recall St. Paul's image of seeing "in a mirror, darkly") but an
excess of illumination. Rather than leaving us blind and in the dark,
this experience would be blinding in another sense. We would be, in

Marion's word, "bedazzled." Saturated phenomena have a double effect: we are made acutely aware of the limits of our own mind, and at the same time, we are made dramatically aware of some reality that vastly exceeds it. For some, this is deeply frustrating; for others, it is profoundly satisfying.

Religious knowing, then, is likely to evoke both humility and gratitude. Humility arises as we acknowledge how little we know about the vast reality extending beyond our meager cognitive powers; gratitude surfaces with a deeper appreciation for what has been manifested to us. Perhaps the most significant religious knowing—often discovered in crises and revisited in community rituals—resists being formulated into rational categories. Instead it thrives best at the intuitive level. Theologian Robert Doran hints at this in his recognition of a "meaning that perhaps forever will be better expressed in the very symbolic, aesthetic, dramatic terms of scripture than in any possible dogmatic clarifications." This suggests that the very effort to categorize intuitive convictions is likely to drain them of vitality.

Today the idolatry of reason associated with the Enlightenment is giving way to a richer appreciation of the remarkable range of human knowing—as well as its enduring limits. This shift opens the way to a renewed recognition of religious intuition and its contribution to human life. Religious appreciation thrives along the broad threshold where reason and emotion overlap, where consciousness contends with the unconscious, where metaphors flourish. In this rich soil religious intuitions and spiritual inspirations thrive.

Additional Resources

For full reference information, consult the Bibliography.

Chapter 1

The quotation that opens this chapter appears in George Vaillant's *Spiritual Evolution: A Scientific Defense of Faith*. See also his essay "Positive Emotions, Spirituality and the Practice of Psychiatry." Martin Seligman's comments are drawn from his essay "Positive Psychology." For Daniel Siegel's perspective, see his chapter "Mindfulness," in *The Science of Optimism and Hope*. See also Kenneth Pargament and Annette Mahoney, "Spirituality: The Search for the Sacred"; and Marvin Levine, *The Positive Psychology of Buddhism and Yoga*.

Thomas Aquinas links moral virtue with passion; see his *Treatise on the Virtues*. Diana Fritz Cates explores emotions as potentially religious in *Aquinas on the Emotions: A Religious-Ethical Inquiry*. James Keenan discusses mercy as a central emotion in Catholic tradition in *Moral Wisdom*. From a Protestant perspective, Robert Roberts discusses the role of emotions in Christian living in *Spiritual Emotions: A Psychology of Christian Virtue*.

Barbara Fredrickson sets out the "broaden and build" theory in *Positivity: How to Embrace the Hidden Strength of Positive Emotions*; for a fuller discussion, see her earlier essay, "Cultivating Positive Emotions to Optimize Health and Well-Being."

Paul Gilbert has written extensively on the three domains of emotional regulation; the chart we include here is modified from his discussion in *The Compassionate Mind*. James Gustafson's definition of dispositions is found in Simon Harak's *Virtuous Passions*. See also John Cottingham, *The Spiritual Dimension: Religion, Philosophy and Human Value*; and Charles Taylor, *A Secular Age*.

Chapter 2

Caroline Bynum examines wonder in *Metamorphosis and Identity*. See also Robert Fuller's discussion in *Wonder: From Emotion to*

Spirituality, and Charles Taylor's definition in *A Secular Age.* Jonathan Haidt discusses the loss of wonder among early scientists in *The Happiness Hypothesis.*

In *The Fragility of Goodness* Martha Nussbaum reflects on the nuances of wonder in ancient Greek literature. Rachel Carson links . wonder to environmental concerns in *Silent Spring.* Elaine Scarry links beauty and wonder in *On Beauty and Being Just.*

Dacher Keltner and Jonathan Haidt explore awe in their essay "Approaching Awe: A Moral, Spiritual and Aesthetic Emotion." Philip Wheelwright describes awe in *Metaphor and Reality.* Robert Alter discusses awe and the story of Job in *The Wisdom Books.*

Susan Neiman examines reverence in *Moral Clarity.* See also Paul Woodruff's discussion in *Reverence: Renewing a Forgotten Virtue.*

George Steiner explores the mysterious aspects of music in *Real Presences.* In *The Divine Proportion: A Study in Mathematical Beauty* H. E. Huntley discusses the wonder evoked by the order in numbers and ratios. See also Ian Barbour, *Myths, Models and Paradigms: A Comparative Study in Science and Religion.*

Chapter 3

Robert Emmons discusses psychology's retrieval of the cognitive function of emotions in *The Psychology of Ultimate Concern.* In *Mindsight* Daniel Siegel reports on emotions' role in information processing. In *Descartes' Error* and elsewhere Antonio Demasio has pioneered research on the cognitive function of emotions. See also Benedict Carey, "In Battle, Hunches Prove to Be Valuable Assets." George Vaillant discusses the evolution of emotions in *Spiritual Evolution;* see also his essay "Positive Emotions, Spirituality and the Practice of Psychiatry."

Robert Solomon's *The Passions: The Myth and Nature of Human Emotions* marks an early recognition of emotions' significance by a contemporary philosopher. Martha Nussbaum is a leader in the effort she has named "the rehabilitation of emotion." From her prolific writing consult especially *Love's Knowledge, Upheavals of Thought, Therapy of Desire* and *Hiding from Humanity.*

Jonathan Haidt provides definitions of the moral emotions in his essay "The Moral Emotions" in *Handbook of Affective Sciences.* See also his chapter, "Elevation and the Positive Psychology of Morality," in *Flourishing: Positive Psychology and the Life Well-Lived.* Dacher Keltner discusses the healing emotions of elevation and laughter in *Born to Be Good.* Susan Neiman discusses moral needs in *Moral*

Clarity. William Spohn considers emotions' contribution to moral theology; see "Passions and Principles," in "Notes on Moral Theology: 1990," in *Theological Studies.*

Richard Sorabji reflects on attitudes toward laughter in the early church in *Emotions and Peace of Mind: From Stoic Agitation to Christian Temptation.* Garrison Keillor recalls his own experience in *Lake Wobegon Days.*

Chapter 4

Annie Dillard discusses would-be "heroic times" in *For the Time Being.* In *Character Strengths and Virtues,* Christopher Peterson and Martin Seligman include bravery, persistence, integrity and vitality in their analysis of the character strength of courage. Josef Pieper examines courage in *The Four Cardinal Virtues.* See also Lee Yearley, *Mencius and Aquinas: Theories of Virtue and Conceptions of Courage.*

For an expanded look at the potentially positive role of anger and fear in the development of courage, see our *Transforming Our Painful Emotions,* especially chapters 5, "An Angry Spirituality," and 13, "The Christian Script for Fear."

Erik Erikson defines and discusses hope in *Insight and Responsibility.* See also C. R. Snyder, *The Psychology of Hope;* and C. R. Snyder and Shane Lopez, "Hope Theory: A Member of the Positive Psychology Family," in *Handbook of Positive Psychology.*

Victoria McGeer's influential article "The Art of Good Hope" appears in *Annals of the American Academy of Politics and Social Science* (March 2004).

Chapter 5

Barbara Fredrickson explores interest and curiosity in "What Good Are Positive Emotions?" Stanley Fish quotes Paul Griffiths's indictment of curiosity in contemporary culture in "Does Curiosity Kill More Than the Cat?" In "Distilling the Wisdom of C.E.O.s," Adam Bryant cites Nell Minow's positive evaluation of "passionate curiosity."

Jodi Halpern argues for the development of "well-cultivated curiosity" as essential to effective therapeutic practice; see *From Detached Curiosity to Empathy: Humanizing Medical Practice.* See also Barbara Benedict, *Curiosity: A Cultural History of Early Modern Inquiry;* and Todd Kashdan, *Curious: Discover the Missing Ingredient to a Fulfilling Life.*

Simon Harak discusses Aquinas's understanding of contentment in *Virtuous Passions*. Thich Nhat Hanh and Lilian Cheung offer practical suggestions for cultivating contentment in *Savor: Mindful Eating, Mindful Life*. See also Patrick McCormick, "A Right to Beauty: A Fair Share of Milk and Honey for the Poor"; and Elaine Scarry, *On Beauty and Being Just*.

Mary Jo Leddy explores the links between the culture and "perpetual dissatisfaction" in *Radical Gratitude*. William Schweiker discusses "culturally saturated desires" in *Having: Property and Possessions in Religious and Social Life*.

Chapter 6

Diana Fritz Cates comments on Aquinas's view of joy in *Aquinas on the Emotions*. See also Daniel Siegel's discussion in *Mindsight;* and Paul Pahil's definition on the Centre for Applied Psychology website. John Mahoney notes Augustine's crucial distinction of *enjoyment* and *use* in *The Making of Moral Theology*.

Martin Seligman has pioneered the investigation of happiness within the Positive Psychology movement. His own position has matured from the earlier discussion in *Authentic Happiness*, through his contributions in *A Life Worth Living*, to an more nuanced discussion in *Flourish: A Visionary New Understanding of Happiness and Well-being*.

For further discussion, see Tai Ben-Shaker, *Happier: Daily Joy and Lasting Fulfillment;* Daniel Gilbert, *Stumbling on Happiness;* Matthieu Ricard and Daniel Goleman, *Happiness: A Guide to Developing Life's Most Important Skill;* and Robert Cloninger, *Feeling Good: The Science of Well Being*.

Paul Ricoeur offers his description of human flourishing in *Oneself as Another*. Charles Taylor discusses human flourishing throughout his significant volume *A Secular Age*. See also Corey Keyes and Jonathan Haidt, eds., *Flourishing: Positive Psychology and the Life Well-Lived*.

Chapter 7

The pioneering work of John Bowlby (Great Britain) and Mary Ainsworth (USA) on psychological attachment has influenced scholars and therapists throughout the English-speaking world. For a readable introduction, see John Bowlby, *A Secure Base: Parent-Child Attachment and Healthy Human Development*.

Daniel Siegel provides an excellent introduction and overview of attachment theory in *The Developing Mind: How Relationships and the*

Brain Interact to Shape Who We Are. For an accessible and insightful examination of the neurological basis of attachment behavior and its significance in human development and maturing love relationships, see Thomas Lewis, Fari Amini and Richard Lannon, *A General Theory of Love.*

We discuss the spiritual and psychological dimensions of love in *Wisdom of the Body: Making Sense of Our Sexuality.* See also Helen Fisher, *Why We Love: The Nature and Chemistry of Romantic Love.*

Psychiatrist Takeo Doi offers the classic analysis of *amae* in *The Anatomy of Dependence.* See also Roberto Unger's *Passion: An Essay on Personality,* in which he discusses the ambivalence of our need for closeness and caution in relationships. John Bayley describes his life with Iris Murdoch in *Elegy for Iris.*

Chapter 8

Erik Erikson describes the emergence of a healthy sense of pride in *Childhood and Society.* Willard Gaylin provides an excellent overview of the psychological dynamics of pride in *Feelings: Our Vital Signs.* Roberto Unger discusses pride in *Passion: An Essay on Personality.* Avis Clendenen examines "the lost art of humility" in "A Rare Humility and a Future-Facing Myth," in *Review for Religious.*

Josef Pieper discusses magnanimity as part of humility in *The Four Cardinal Virtues.* Historian of philosophy Anthony Kenny comments on Aquinas's discussion in *A New History of Western Philosophy.* See also Lisa Fullam, *The Virtue of Humility;* and Brian Daley, "'To Be More like Christ.' The Background and Implications of Three Kinds of Humility," in *Studies in the Spirituality of Jesuits.*

Chapter 9

Phyllis Trible examines compassion in the Hebrew scriptures in *God and the Rhetoric of Sexuality.* Anindita Balslev and Dirk Evers provide a compelling overview of interfaith dimensions in *Compassion in the World's Religions: Envisioning Human Solidarity.*

Dacher Keltner explores compassion as a body-based response in *Born to Be Good: The Science of a Meaningful Life.* Paul Gilbert discusses the neuropsychological basis of compassion, as well as the development and expression of this human strength, in *The Compassionate Mind: A New Approach to Life's Challenges.* See also Bryan Stone, *Compassionate Ministry: Theological Foundations;* and Diana Fritz Cates, *Choosing to Feel: Virtue, Friendship and Compassion for Friends.*

Daniel Siegel discusses "resonance" in *Mindsight*. In *Moral Minds: The Nature of Right and Wrong*, Marc Hauser presents current research findings on the role of empathy in moral development. For discussions of the contemporary significance of religious and moral practices, see Alasdair MacIntyre, *After Virtue*; Dorothy Bass, *Practicing Our Faith*; and Stephanie Paulsell, *Honoring the Body: Meditations on a Christian Practice*.

James Keenan explores the virtue of self-care in *Virtues for Ordinary Christians* and again in *Moral Wisdom*. See also Kristin Neff's discussion in *Self-Compassion: A Healthier Way of Relating to Yourself*; and Christopher Gerner's *The Mindful Path to Self-Compassion*.

Chapter 10

J. Warren Smith provides a rich consideration of Gregory of Nyssa's theology in *Passion and Paradise: Human and Divine Emotion in the Thought of Gregory of Nyssa*. Boyd Taylor Coolman comments on "a certain patristic reserve" in his essay, "Hugh of St. Victor on 'Jesus Wept': Compassion as Ideal *Humanitas*." In *Cosmopolis*, Stephen Toulmin notes the shift from sixteenth-century humanism to a seventeenth-century mood of intolerance.

James O'Donnell offers a critical analysis in *Augustine: A New Biography*. Martha Nussbaum provides further insight into Augustine's view of the emotions in *Upheavals of Thought: The Intelligence of the Emotions*. She discusses vulnerability in *Hiding from Humanity: Disgust, Shame and the Law*.

Peter Brown reflects on Jerome's influence in Christian interpretations of the flesh in *Body and Society*. In *Quest for the Living God* Elizabeth Johnson reviews the ideal of God as removed from all emotion and suffering. Charles Taylor introduces "excarnation" in *A Secular Age*.

On the early development of moral theology, see John Mahoney, *The Making of Moral Theology*; and Norbert Rigali "From 'Moral Theology' to the 'Theology of the Christian Life': An Overview."

Chapter 11

For Aquinas's exploration of the relation of passion to virtue, see *Treatise on the Virtues*. See also Peter Brown's discussion in *Body and Society*.

Roberto Unger explores the ennobling passions in *Passion: An Essay on Personality*. See also George Vaillant, *Spiritual Evolution: A Scientific Defense of Faith*.

Matthew Elliott examines biblical perspectives on emotions in *Faithful Feelings: Emotion in the New Testament*.

Erik Erikson discusses the human capacity for hope in several places; see, for example, *Toys and Reasons* and *Identity: Youth and Crisis*. Monika Hellwig includes hope in her entry, "Eschatology," in *Systematic Theology: Volume Two*. See also Anthony Scioli and Henry Biller, *Hope in an Age of Anxiety*.

Paul Ricoeur's discussion of sexuality, "Wonder, Eroticism, and Enigma," is available in *Sexuality and the Sacred: Sources for Theological Reflection*.

Chapter 12

Lewis Hyde explores the dynamics of gift giving in *The Gift: Imagination and the Erotic Life of Property*. Georg Simmel defines gratitude in his essay "Faithfulness and Gratitude," in *The Sociology of Georg Simmel*. Philip Watkins reviews recent research findings on the positive emotion of gratitude in "Gratitude and Subjective Well-Being,"in *The Psychology of Gratitude*. See also Charles Shelton, *The Gratitude Factor: Enhancing Your Life through Grateful Living*.

Margaret Visser's discussion of gratitude is found in *The Gift of Thanks: The Roots and Rituals of Gratitude*. In *Radical Gratitude*, Mary Jo Leddy examines tensions between culturally induced dissatisfaction and the emergence of gratitude. Wilkie Au and Noreen Cannon Au, in *The Grateful Heart*, reinforce the role of gratitude in living out the Christian message.

George Vaillant describes forgiveness in *Spiritual Evolution: A Scientific Defense of Faith*. See also Marjorie Hewitt Suchocki's exploration of forgiveness in *The Fall to Violence*. Paul Ricoeur discusses forgiveness at both the personal and institutional levels in *Memory, History, Forgetting*. Avis Clendenen and Troy Martin highlight the dynamics of the "forgiveness exchange" in *Forgiveness: Finding Freedom through Reconciliation*.

Chapter 13

Robert C. Roberts presents "Justice as an Emotion Disposition" in *Emotion Review*. In *The Compassionate Mind* Paul Gilbert distinguishes physiological and psychological dynamics that are part of "restorative justice" and "retributive justice." These themes are expanded by Martha Nussbaum in *Frontiers of Justice* and by Michael Sandel in *Justice*.

David Hollenbach examines justice and solidarity in relation to the common good in *The Common Good and Christian Ethics*. For further discussion of the common good, see John Coleman, "Pluralism and the Retrieval of a Catholic Sense of the Common Good"; and E. J. Dionne, "Faith, Politics, and the Common Good," in *Religion and Values in Public Life*.

In *The Beatitude of Mercy* Terry Veling provides a comprehensive examination of the biblical understanding of mercy, with compelling implications for pastoral response. See also Heather Chappell's evocative discussion in her paper for the Catholic Theological Society (2001), "Conversion by Mercy and For a Praxis of Mercy."

Chapter 14

European scholars Jean Danielou, Henri du Lubac and Hans Urs von Balthasar pioneered the retrieval of the Eastern theological tradition as a resource for Western Christianity. Warren Smith comments on the fruitful results of this cross-fertilization in *Passion and Paradise: Human and Divine Emotion in the Thought of Gregory of Nyssa*.

See also Melvin Laird, "Under Solomon's Tutelage: The Education of Desire in the Homilies on the Song of Songs," in *Re-thinking Gregory of Nyssa*; and Sarah Coakley, "Pleasure Principles—Toward a Contemporary Theology of Desire."

Peter C. Hill is past president of Division 36 (Psychology of Religion) of the American Psychological Association. "Spiritual Transformation: Forming the Habitual Center of Personal Energy" is the text of his presidential address, delivered August 26, 2001. William James explores psychological dynamics in the experience of religious faith in *Varieties of Religious Experience*. Michael Paul Gallagher discusses the rhythm of consolation and desolation in *Clashing Symbols*.

Chapter 15

British psychologist Adam Phillips explores religion in his essay "A Mind Is a Terrible Thing to Measure." In *Real Presences* George Steiner examines the extra-rational knowledge transmitted in music and other art forms. Richard Shweder writes of alternate ways of knowing in the Introduction to *Thinking through Cultures: Expeditions in Cultural Psychology*.

British philosopher John Cottingham describes the limits of human knowledge in *The Spiritual Dimension: Religion, Philosophy and Human Value*. See also David Myer, *Intuition: Its Powers and Perils*.

Art critic Peter Schjeldahl analyzes the extraordinary power of El Greco's work in his essay, "El Greco at the Met." Gerd Gigerenzer explores "the intelligence of the unconscious" in *Gut Feeling*.

Jean-Luc Marion discusses his understanding of "saturated phenomenon" in *Phenomenology and the Theological Turn* and in *Excess: Studies of Saturated Phenomena*. See also William Connolly, "Catholicism and Philosophy, a Nontheistic Appreciation"; Paul Avis's discussion in *God and the Creative Imagination*; and Robert Doran, "What Is Systematic Theology?"

The Vocabulary
of Healing Emotions

In these chapters we have explored the *emotions* of joy, compassion, wonder, curiosity, awe. The longer-lasting affects—contentment, happiness, hope—we discussed as *moods*. Included, too, were resources traditionally named *virtues*—courage, pride, humility, mercy—and others, such as justice, forgiveness, gratitude, typically referred to as dispositions or *character traits*. The psychological categories of empathy, interest and appreciation were considered to be *evolved capacities*.

The positive psychology movement has not reached general agreement on the terms to be used to identify these different positive experiences. And discussion continues about which experiences should be listed within each category. So we offer here *working definitions* of several of the terms we have used throughout the book, confident that readers will be able to make sense of these slightly different vocabulary choices.

Emotion: A discrete feeling or affect—such as fear, joy, compassion. In current research an *emotion* is understood to involve three aspects: (a) physiological arousal; (b) cognitive interpretation; and (c) behavioral response (often some kind of action).

Mood: An enduring emotional state—usually understood as a more passive experience, less a result of personal choice or active development than is a disposition.

Disposition: A general orientation or cultivated attitude toward particular behaviors. Theologian James Gustafson writes: "By disposition I wish to suggest *a manner of life, a lasting or persisting tendency, a bearing toward one another and the world, a readiness to act in a certain way.*"

Virtue (as discussed by psychologists such as Erik Erikson): This term points to inherent personality resources, such as trust and intimacy that—when developed—support human flourishing.

Virtue (as discussed by theologians such as Thomas Aquinas): This term points to personal resources like faith and courage that are understood as God-given strengths that also require personal effort for development.

Passion: This term has ambiguous meaning in Christian history, often pointing to overwhelming or destructive feelings (rage, phobias, sexual excess) but also used to designate strong or compelling positive feelings (passionate love or devotion, com-passion).

Evolved capacities: In psychological research the term *evolved capacities* is used to identify resources—such as empathy, trust, generosity—that are evident in primate behavior and have expanded in our species into cognitive and emotional abilities that shape a life of human flourishing.

Practices: The term is used today to point to intentional actions that are performed regularly with the effect of strengthening moral character, for example, practices of friendship, hospitality, forgiveness, civic participation.

Enabling institutions: These are communities and organizations that promote human flourishing and foster the development of character strengths. Included here are stable families, educational and civic organizations, support groups, parishes and, more generally, religion as *a school of the emotions.*

Bibliography

Alter, Robert. *The Wisdom Books: Job, Proverts, and Ecclesiastes: A Translation with Commentary* (New York: W. W. Norton and Company, 2010).

Aquinas, Thomas. *Summa Theologica*. Translated by Fathers of the English Dominican Province. Westminster, MD: Christian Classics, 1981.

———. *Treatise on the Virtues*. Translated by John A. Oesterle. Notre Dame, IN: University of Notre Dame Press, 1966.

Aristotle. *The Basic Works of Aristotle*. Edited by Richard McKeon. New York: Random House, 1941.

———. *Nicomachean Ethics*. Edited by Robert Bartlett and Susan Collins. Chicago: University of Chicago Press, 2011.

Avis, Paul. *God and the Creative Imagination: Metaphor, Symbol and Myth in Religion and Theology*. London: Routledge, 1999.

Au, Wilkie, and Noreen Cannon Au. *The Grateful Heart: Living the Christian Message*. New York: Paulist Press, 2011.

Balslev, Anindita, and Dirk Evers, eds. *Compassion in the World's Religions: Envisioning Human Solidarity*. Berlin: LIT Verlag Publishers, 2010.

Bass, Dorothy. *Practicing Our Faith*. San Francisco: Jossey-Bass, 1997.

Barbour, Ian. *Myths, Models and Paradigms: A Comparative Study in Science and Religion*. New York: Harper and Row, 1974.

Baumeister, Roy. "Rethinking Self-Esteem." *Stanford Social Innovation Review* (Winter 2005): 34-41.

Bayley, John. *Elegy for Iris*. New York: Picador, 1999.

Beaudoin, Tom. *Consuming Faith: Integrating Who We Are with What We Buy*. Lanham, MD: Sheed and Ward, 2003.

Benedict, Barbara. *Curiosity: A Cultural History of Early Modern Inquiry*. Chicago: University of Chicago Press, 2001.

Ben-Shaker, Tai. *Happier: Daily Joy and Lasting Fulfillment*. McGraw-Hill, 2007.

Bowlby, John. *A Secure Base: Parent-Child Attachment and Healthy Human Development*. New York: Basic Books, 1988.

Brooks, David. "The End of Philosophy." *The New York Times*. April 6, 2009.

———. "The Empathy Issue." *The New York Times*. May 29, 2009.

Brown, Peter. *Augustine of Hippo: A Biography*. Berkeley and Los Angeles: University of California Press, 1967.

———. *Body and Society: Men, Women and Sexual Renunciation in Early Christianity*. New York: Columbia University Press, 1988.

Bryant, Adam. "Distilling the Wisdom of C.E.O.s." *The New York Times.* April 17, 2011.

Bynum, Caroline. *Metamorphosis and Identity*, Cambridge, MA: MIT Press, 2001.

Carey, Benedict. "In Battle, Hunches Prove to Be Valuable Assets." *The New York Times.* July 28, 2009.

Carson, Rachel. *Silent Spring.* Boston, MA: Houghton Mifflin, 1962.

Cates, Diana Fritz. *Aquinas on the Emotions: A Religious-Ethical Inquiry.* Washington DC: Georgetown University Press, 2009.

Chappell, Heather. "Conversion by Mercy and for a Praxis of Mercy." Paper delivered at the 2001 annual meeting of the Catholic Theological Society of America.

Clendenen, Avis. "A Rare Humility and a Future-Facing Myth." *Review for Religious* 69, no. 3 (2010): 268-80.

Clendenen, Avis, and Troy Martin. *Forgiveness: Finding Freedom through Reconciliation.* New York: Crossroad, 2002.

Cloninger, C. Robert. *Feeling Good: The Science of Well-Being.* New York: Oxford University Press, 2004.

Coakley, Sarah. "Pleasure Principles—Toward a Contemporary Theology of Desire." *Harvard Divinity Bulletin* (Autumn 2005): 17-31.

Coolman, Boyd Taylor. "Hugh of St. Victor on 'Jesus Wept': Compassion as Ideal *Humanitas.*" *Theological Studies* 69 (2008): 528-56.

Cotter, James. *Homosexual and Holy.* Available on the way.org.uk website.

Cottingham, John. *The Spiritual Dimension: Religion, Philosophy and Human Value.* Cambridge: Cambridge University Press, 2005.

Csikszentmihalyi, Isabella, ed. *A Life Worth Living: Perspectives from Positive Psychology.* New York: Oxford University Press, 2004.

Daley, Brian. "'To Be More like Christ.' The Background and Implications of 'Three Kinds of Humility.'" *Studies in the Spirituality of Jesuits* 27, no. 1 (January 2009).

Demasio, Antonio. *Descartes' Error: Emotion, Reason and the Human Brain.* San Francisco: HarperCollins, 1994.

Dillard, Annie. *For the Time Being.* New York: Knopf, 1999.

Dionne, E. J. "Faith, Politics and the Common Good." *Religion and Values in Public Life* 6, no. 2 (Spring 1998): 2-3.

Doi, Takeo. *The Anatomy of Dependence.* Tokyo: Kodansha International, 1973.

Doran, Robert. "What Is Systematic Theology?" Quoted in Thomas Hughson, "Interpreting Vatican II: 'A New Pentecost.'" *Theological Studies* 69 (2008).

Elliott, Matthew. *Faithful Feelings: Emotion in the New Testament.* Nottingham, UK: Inter-Varsity Press, 2005.

Emmons, Robert. *The Psychology of Ultimate Concern: Motivation and Spirituality in Personality.* New York: Guilford Press, 1999.

Emmons, Robert, and Michael McCullough, eds. *The Psychology of Gratitude.* New York: Oxford University Press, 2004.

Epstein, Mark. *Open to Desire: The Truth about What the Buddha Taught.* New York: Penguin, 2005.

Erikson, Erik. *Childhood and Society.* New York: Norton, 1963.

———. *Identity: Youth and Crisis.* New York: Norton, 1968.

———. *Insight and Responsibility.* New York: Norton, 1964.

———. *Toys and Reasons.* New York: Norton, 1977.

Fish, Stanley. "Does Curiosity Kill More Than the Cat?" *The New York Times.* September 14, 2009.

Fisher, Helen. *Why We Love: The Nature and Chemistry of Romantic Love.* New York: Holt, 2004.

Fredrickson, Barbara. *Positivity: Groundbreaking Research Reveals How to Embrace the Hidden Strength of Positive Emotions, Overcome Negativity and Thrive.* New York: Crown Books, 2009.

———. "Cultivating Positive Emotions to Optimize Health and Well-Being." *Prevention and Treatment.* Volume 3. Article 0001a. Posted March 7, 2000. Copyright 2000 by the American Psychological Association.

Fullam, Lisa. *The Virtue of Humility.* Lewiston, NY: The Edwin Mellon Press, 2009.

Fuller, Robert. *Wonder: From Emotion to Spirituality.* Chapel Hill: University of North Carolina Press, 2006.

Gallagher, Michael Paul. *Clashing Symbols.* New York: Paulist Press, 1998.

Gaylin, Willard. *Feelings: Our Vital Signs.* New York: Harper and Row, 1989.

Gerner, Christopher. *The Mindful Path to Self-Compassion.* New York: Guilford Press, 2009.

Gigerenzr, Gerd. *Gut Feeling: The Intelligence of the Unconscious* (London: Penguin Books, 2007).

Gilbert, Daniel. *Stumbling on Happiness.* New York: Harper Perennial, 2007.

Gilbert, Paul. *The Compassionate Mind.* Oakland, CA: New Harbinger Publications, 2009.

Haidt, Jonathan. "Elevation and the Positive Psychology of Morality." In *Flourishing: Positive Psychology and the Life Well-Lived*, ed. C. L. M. Keyes and J. Haidt, 275-89. Washington DC: American Psychological Association, 2003.

———. "The Moral Emotions." In *Handbook of Affective Sciences*, ed. R. J. Davidson, K. R. Scherer and H. H Goldsmith, 852-70. Oxford: Oxford University Press, 2003.

———. *The Happiness Hypothesis.* New York: Basic Books, 2006.

———, and Dacher Keltner, "Approaching Awe: A Moral, Spiritual and Aesthetic Emotion." *Cognition and Emotion* 17 (2003): 297-314.

Hanh, Thich Nhat, and Lilian Cheung. *Savor: Mindful Eating, Mindful Life.* New York: HarperCollins, 2010.

Halpern, Jodi. *From Detached Curiosity to Empathy: Humanizing Medical Practice.* New York: Oxford University Press, 2011.

Harak, Simon. *Virtuous Passions.* New York: Paulist Press, 1993.

Hauser, Marc. *Moral Minds: The Nature of Right and Wrong.* New York: HarperCollins, 2006.

Hellwig, Monika. "Eschatology." In *Systematic Theology*, vol. 2, ed. Francis Schussler Fiorenza and John Galvin. Minneapolis: Fortress Press, 1991.

Hill, Peter C. "Spiritual Transformation: Forming the Habitual Center of Personal Energy." Presidential address to the Psychology of Religion and Spirituality Division of the American Psychological Association. August 26, 2001.

Hollenbach, David. *The Common Good and Christian Ethics*. New York: Cambridge University Press, 2002.

Huntley, H. E. *The Divine Proportion: A Study in Mathematical Beauty*. New York: Dover Publications, 1970.

Hyde, Lewis. *The Gift: Imagination and the Erotic Life of Property*. New York: Random House, 1983.

Johnson, Elizabeth. *Quest for the Living God*. New York: Continuum, 2007.

Kashdan, Todd. *Curious: Discover the Missing Ingredient to a Fulfilling Life*. New York: Wm. Morrow, 2009.

Keenan, James. *Moral Wisdom*. New York: Rowman and Littlefield, 2004.

———. *Virtues for Ordinary Christians*. Kansas City, MO: Sheed and Ward, 1996.

Keillor, Garrison. *Lake Wobegon Days*. New York: Viking Press, 1985.

Keltner, Dacher. *Born to Be Good: The Science of a Meaningful Life*. New York: Norton, 2009.

Kenny, Anthony. *A New History of Western Philosophy*. Oxford: Oxford University Press, 2007.

Keyes, Corey, and Jonathan Haidt, eds. *Flourishing: Positive Psychology and the Life Well-Lived*. Washington DC: American Psychological Association, 2003.

Laird, Melvin. "Under Solomon's Tutelage: Education of Desire in the Homilies on the Song of Songs." In *Rethinking Gregory of Nyssa*, ed. Sarah Coakley. Oxford: Blackwell, 2003.

Leddy, Mary Jo. *Radical Gratitude*. Maryknoll, NY: Orbis Books, 2002.

Leon-Dufour, Xavier. *Dictionary of Biblical Theology*. New York: Crossroad, 1973.

Levine, Marvin. *The Positive Psychology of Buddhism and Yoga*. Lawrence Erlbaum, 2000.

Lewis, Thomas, Fari Amini and Richard Lannon. *A General Theory of Love*. New York: Vintage, 2001.

MacIntyre, Alasdair. *After Virtue*. Notre Dame, IN: University of Notre Dame Press, 1981.

Mahoney, John. *The Making of Moral Theology*. New York: Oxford University Press, 1987.

Mamet, David. "Attention Must Be Paid." *The New York Times*. February 13, 2005.

Marion, Jean-Luc. "The Saturated Phenomenon." In *Phenomenology and the Theological Turn*, ed. Dominique Janicaud, Jean-Francois Courtine, Jen-Louis Chretien, Michel Henry Jean-Luc Marion and Paul Ricoeur. New York: Fordham University Press, 2000.

McCormick, Patrick. "A Right to Beauty: A Fair Share of Milk and Honey for the Poor." *Theological Studies* 71 (2010): 702–20.

McGeer, Victoria. "The Art of Good Hope." In *Hope, Power and Governance.* Special issue of Annals of American Academy of Political and Social Science, vol. 592 (March 2004): 100-127.

Miles, Margaret. *Desire and Delight: A New Reading of Augustine's Confessions.* New York: Crossroad, 1992.

Myers, David. *Intuition: Its Powers and Perils* (New Haven, CT: Yale University Press, 2002).

Neff, Kristin. *Self-Compassion: A Healthier Way of Relating to Yourself.* New York: HarperCollins, 2011.

Neiman, Susan. *Moral Clarity.* Princeton, NJ: Princeton University Press, 2009.

Nussbaum, Martha. *Frontiers of Justice.* Cambridge, MA: Harvard University Press, 2006.

———. *Hiding from Humanity: Disgust, Shame and the Law.* Princeton, NJ: Princeton University Press, 2004.

———. *Love's Knowledge.* New York: Oxford University Press, 1990.

———. *The Fragility of Goodness: Luck and Ethics in Greek Tragedy and Philosophy.* Revised edition. Cambridge: Cambridge University Press, 2001.

———. *Therapy of Desire.* Princeton, NJ: Princeton University Press, 1994.

———. *Upheavals of Thought: The Intelligence of Emotions.* Cambridge: Cambridge University Press, 2001.

O'Donnell, James. *Augustine, A New Biography.* New York: HarperCollins, 2005.

Pargament, Kenneth, and Annette Mahoney. "Spirituality: The Search for the Sacred." In *Oxford Handbook of Positive Psychology,* 2nd ed., ed. Shane J. Lopez and C. R. Snyder, 611-20. New York: Oxford University Press, 2009.

Paulsell, Stephanie. *Honoring the Body: Meditations on a Christian Practice.* San Francisco: Jossey-Bass, 2002.

Peterson, Christopher, and Martin Seligman. *Character Strengths and Virtues: A Handbook and Classification.* New York: Oxford University Press, 2004.

Pieper, Josef. *The Four Cardinal Virtues.* Notre Dame, IN: University of Notre Dame Press, 1966.

Plutarch. *On Love, the Family and the Good Life: Selected Essays of Plutarch.* Translated by Moses Hadas. New York: Mentor Books, 1957.

Ricard, Matthieu, and Daniel Goleman. *Happiness: A Guide to Developing Life's Most Important Skill.* Boston: Little Brown, 2007.

Ricoeur, Paul. *Memory, History, Forgetting.* Chicago: University of Chicago Press, 2004.

————. *Oneself as Another.* Chicago: University of Chicago Press, 1992.

————. "Wonder, Eroticism and Enigma." In *Sexuality and the Sacred: Sources for Theological Reflection,* ed. James Nelson and Sandra Longfellow, 8-84. Louisville, KY: Westminster/John Knox, 1994.

Rigali, Norbert. "From 'Moral Theology' to the 'Theology of Christian Life': An Overview." *Origins* (June 24, 2002): 85-91.

Roberts, Robert C. *Spiritual Emotions: A Psychology of Christian Virtue.* Grand Rapids, MI: Eerdmans, 2007.

————. "Justice as an Emotion Disposition." *Emotion Review* 2, no. 1 (January 2010): 36-43.

Sandel, Michael. *Justice: What's the Right Thing to Do?* New York: Farrar, Straus and Giroux, 2009.

Scarry, Elaine. *On Beauty and Being Just.* Princeton, NJ: Princeton University Press, 1999.

Schjeldahl, Peter. "El Greco at the Met." *The New Yorker.* October 20, 2003.

Schmidt, Leigh Erik. "Practices of Exchange: From Market Culture to Gift Economy in the Interpretation of American Religion." In *Lived Religion,* ed. David Hall, 69-91. Princeton, NJ: Princeton University Press, 1997.

Schweiker, William, and C. Mathewes, eds. *Having: Property and Possessions in Religious and Social Life.* Grand Rapids, MI: Eerdmans, 2004.

Scioli, Anthony, and Henry Biller. *Hope in an Age of Anxiety.* New York: Oxford University Press, 2009.

Seligman, Martin. *Authentic Happiness: Using the New Positive Psychology.* New York: Free Press, 2004.

————. *Flourish: A Visionary New Understanding of Happiness and Well-being.* New York: Free Press, 2011.

————. "Positive Psychology." In *The Science of Optimism and Hope,* ed. Jan Gillham. Philadelphia: Templeton Foundation Press, 2000.

Shelton, Charles. *The Gratitude Factor: Enhancing Your Life through Grateful Living.* New York: Paulist Press, 2011.

Shweder, Richard. "Introduction: The Astonishment of Anthropology." In *Thinking through Cultures: Expeditions in Cultural Psychology,* ed. Richard Shweder, 1-23. Cambridge, MA: Harvard University Press, 1991.

Siegel, Daniel. *Mindsight.* New York: Bantam Books, 2010.

————. "Mindfulness." In *The Science of Optimism and Hope,* ed. Jan Gillham. Philadelphia: Templeton Foundation Press, 2000.

————. *The Developing Mind: How Relationships and the Brain Interact to Shape Who We Are.* New York: Guilford Press, 1999.

Simmel, Georg. "Faithfulness and Gratitude." In *The Sociology of Georg Simmel.* New York: Free Press, 1950.

Smith, J. Warren. *Passion and Paradise: Human and Divine Emotion in the Thought of Gregory of Nyssa.* New York: Crossroad, 2004.

Snyder, C. R. *The Psychology of Hope.* New York: Free Press, 1994.

Snyder, C. R., and Shane Lopez. "Hope Theory: A Member of the Positive Psychology Family." In *Handbook of Positive Psychology*. New York: Oxford University Press, 2002.

Solomon, Robert. *The Passions: The Myth and Nature of Human Emotions*. Notre Dame, IN: Notre Dame University Press, 1983.

Sorabji, Richard. *Emotions and Peace of Mind: From Stoic Agitation to Christian Temptation*. New York: Oxford University Press, 2000.

Spohn, William. "Passions and Principles." In "Notes on Moral Theology: 1990." *Theological Studies* 52 (1991): 69-87.

Steiner, George. *Real Presences*. Chicago: University of Chicago Press, 1989.

Sternberg, Esther. *The Balance Within: The Science Connecting Health and Emotions*. New York: W. H. Freeman, 2009.

Stone, Bryan. *Compassionate Ministry: Theological Foundations*. Maryknoll, NY: Orbis Books, 1996.

Suchocki, Marjorie Hewitt. *The Fall to Violence*. New York: Continuum, 1995.

Taylor, Charles. *A Secular Age*. Cambridge, MA: Harvard University Press, 2007.

Toulmin, Stephen. *Cosmopolis: The Hidden Agenda of Modernity*. Chicago: University of Chicago Press, 1990.

Trible, Phyllis. *God and the Rhetoric of Sexuality*. Philadelphia: Fortress Press, 1978.

Unger, Roberto. *Passion: An Essay on Personality*. New York: Free Press, 1984.

Vaillant, George. *Spiritual Evolution: A Scientific Defense of Faith*. New York: Broadway Books, 2008.

———. "Positive Emotions, Spirituality and the Practice of Psychiatry." *Mental Health, Spirituality, Mind* 6 (2008): 48-62.

Veling, Terry. *The Beatitude of Mercy*. Mulgrave, Victoria: John Garrett Publishing, 2010.

Visser, Margaret. *The Gift of Thanks: The Roots and Rituals of Gratitude*. Boston: Houghton Mifflin Harcourt, 2009.

Watkins, Philip. "Gratitude and Subjective Well-being." In *The Psychology of Gratitude,* ed. Robert Emmons and Michael McCullough. New York: Oxford University Press, 2004.

Wheelwright, Philip. *Metaphor and Reality*. Bloomington: Indiana University Press, 1968.

Whitehead, Evelyn Eaton, and James D. Whitehead. *Transforming Our Painful Emotions*. Maryknoll, NY: Orbis Books, 2010.

———. *Wisdom of the Body: Making Sense of Our Sexuality*. New York: Crossroad, 2001.

Woodruff, Paul. *Reverence: Renewing a Forgotten Virtue*. New York: Oxford University Press, 2001.

Yearley, Lee. *Mencius and Aquinas: Theories of Virtue and Conceptions of Courage*. Albany: State University of New York, 1990.

Index

1 Corinthians, 77, 82–83, 85, 109, 147
1 John, 79
1 Kings, 88
1 Timothy, 79
2 Corinthians, 77, 79, 82–83, 98

Alter, Robert, 17
amae, 71–72
Amos, Book of, 128
anger, 5, 26
    and courage, 34, 35–36
    God and, 98
Antigone (Sophocles), 14, 30
anxiety, 5, 34
appreciation, 5, 7, 47–49
Aquinas, Thomas
    on emotions, 4, 101, 109–10
    on contentment, 49
    on courage, 35, 37, 38–39
    on curiosity, 45–46
    on humility, 84–85
    on joy, 57–58
    on pride, 26
Aristotle, 29, 30, 62
Arjuna, 19
attachment, 65–76. *See also* love
Augustine, 26, 29, 45, 50, 51, 58, 80, 99–100, 138–39
Avis, Paul, 153
awe, 12, 17–20
    in the Bible, 17–18
    and fear, 19–20
    and gratitude, 119
    and reverence, 20–21

Barbour, Ian, 21
Bayley, John, 76
Beaudoin, Tom, 51
beauty, 15–16, 48–49
Benedict, Barbara, 46
Bhagavad Gita, 19
bodhisattva, 87
Brooks, David, 28
Brown, Peter, 100
Brueggemann, Walter, 115
Bynum, Caroline Walker, 13

calming systems, 10
Calvin, John, 102
Carson, Rachel, 15
Cates, Diana Fritz, 11, 58
catharsis, 29–30
Chappell, Heather, 132
charity. *See* love
Cheung, Lilian, 47–48
Cimabue, 100–1
Clendenen, Avis, 83
compassion, 5, 6, 7, 9–10, 12, 87–94
    God and, 98
    Jesus and, 87
    and mercy, 135
    practice of, 91–92
    self-, 92–96
Compassionate Mind, The (Gilbert), 8–10
Confessions, The (Augustine), 45, 99
consolation, 143–45
consumerism, 50–51

contentment, 7, 49–51
Cotter, James, 75
Cottingham, John, 11, 148
courage, 33–39, 42
    and anger, 34, 35–36
    Aquinas on, 35, 37, 38–39
    and fear, 34–35
    and hope, 39–42
    and Jesus, 33–34
    and magnanimity, 85
curiosity, 43–47
    Aquinas on, 45–46
    Augustine on, 45
Curly Pyjama Letters (Leunig), 51

Dalai Lama, 87
Demasio, Antonio, 23
Descartes, René, 102
desolation, 143–45
development, psychology of, 65–69,
    78, 89–90
devotion, 75–76
Dillard, Annie, 33
Doi, Takeo, 71–72
Doran, Robert, 155

Elegy for Iris (Bayley), 76
elevation, 26–27
Emmaus story, 35, 117
Emmons, Robert, 23, 31
Emotions
    Aquinas on, 4, 101, 109–10
    changes in, 97–105
    God and, 17, 70, 97–99, 104–5
    healing, 5, 6–11, 27
    and Jesus, 4, 11, 17–18, 33–34,
        57, 77, 79, 98–99
    and liturgy, 11, 16, 59, 120–21
    moral, 25–30
    painful, 5, 7–8
    Paul on, 24, 36, 49, 70, 77, 79,
        82–83, 98–9
    positive, 6, 7–8
    in Psalms, 3, 13, 17, 55, 65,
        97–98

and reason, 23–25, 103, 148–55
    regulation of, 8–10
    and religion, 11–12
empathy, 89–90
Ephesians, Letter to the, 36
Erikson, Erik, 39, 75, 78, 111

faith, 109, 111, 114–15
    and hope, 41–42
    and love, 111
fear, 5, 19–20
    and courage, 34–35
fidelity, 75–76
flourishing, human, 62–64
    courage and, 37–39
forgiveness, 124–26
Francis of Assisi, 101
Fredrickson, Barbara, 7–8, 43–44,
    49, 110–11
Freud, Sigmund, 4
Fuller, Robert, 13–14

Galatians, Letter to the, 82
Gallagher, Michael Paul, 144–45
Gaylin, Willard, 77, 78, 85
generosity, 123–24
    Jesus and, 124
Genesis, 72, 117
gift-giving, 121–24. *See also* grati-
    tude
Gigerenzer, Gerd, 149, 150–51
Gilbert, Daniel, 114
Gilbert, Paul, 8–10, 135–36
goal-seeking systems, 8–9
God
    and anger, 98
    and awe, 17
    and compassion, 98
    and emotions, 17, 70, 97–99,
        104–5
    and jealousy, 70
    and mercy, 133
gratitude, 6, 8, 119–23
    and awe, 119. *See also* gift-giving
Gregory of Nyssa, 100, 137–38

grief, 5
Griffiths, Paul, 45–46
guilt, 5

Hahn, Thich Nhat, 47–48
Haidt, Jonathan, 17, 18–20, 25, 26, 27
Halpern, Jodi, 44
happiness, 55, 58–62
Harak, Simon, 49
Hauser, Marc, 89–90
healing emotions, 5, 6–11, 27
Hellwig, Monika, 116
Hill, Peter, 139–43
Hollenbach, David, 130–31
hope, 6, 7, 12, 28–29, 109, 111–
    113, 115–16
    and courage, 39–42
    and faith, 41–42
    and religion, 41–42
humility, 83–86
    and magnanimity, 84–85
    and temperance, 85
Huntley, H.E., 16
Hyde, Lewis, 120, 121

Ignatius of Loyola, 101, 137,
    143–44
imagination, 114–17
Irenaeus, ix, 80
Isaiah, Book of, 7, 12, 58, 114, 115

James, William, 139–40, 148–49
Jealousy
    God and, 70
    and love, 113–14
Jerome, 45
Jesus
    and compassion, 87
    and courage, 33–34
    and emotions, 4, 11, 17–18,
        33–34, 57, 77, 79, 98–99
    and generosity, 124
    and joy, 57
    and love, 116–17
    and pride, 77, 79

Job, Book of, 17, 97
John of the Cross, 101
John, Gospel of, 37, 57, 99
John Paul II, 131
Johnson, Elizabeth, 104
joy, 6, 55–58
    in Bible, 57
justice, 127–32, 134, 135–36
    and mercy, 127, 133–34

Keenan, James, 6, 94–96, 133
Keillor, Garrison, 29, 46–47
Keltner, Dacher, 17, 18–20, 28, 29,
    88
Kenny, Anthony, 84
Kuhn, Thomas, 14

Lahr, John, 29, 151–52
Laird, Melvin, 138
laughter, 29, 56, 99–100
Leddy, Mary Jo, 50
Leon-Dufour, Xavier, 82
Leunig, Michael, 51
liturgy, and emotions, 11, 16, 59,
    120–21
love, 5, 7, 109, 113–14, 116–17
    and attachment, 65–76
    and faith, 111
    Jesus and, 116–17
Luke, Gospel of, 18, 34 56, 79,
    83–84, 94, 119
    Emmaus story in, 35, 117
lust, 113
Luther, Martin, 101–2

magnanimity, 84–85
    and courage, 85
Magnificat, 83–84
Marion, Jean-Luc, 153–55
Mark, Gospel of, 18, 34, 116
Matthew, Gospel of, 18, 34, 57, 79,
    123, 133
McCormick, Patrick, 48
McGeer, Victoria, 40
Meister Eckhart, 122

Mencius, 37, 50, 87
mercy, 6, 127, 128, 132–36
    and compassion, 135
    God and, 133
Micah, Book of, 127
Minow, Neil, 44
moral emotions, 25–30
Murdoch, Irish, 76
Myers, David, 149–50

Neff, Kristin, 93
Neiman, Susan, 8, 25–26, 27–28,
    86, 148
Nussbaum, Martha, 14, 23–24, 30,
    37, 62–63, 104, 129

Oedipus, 30

Pahil, Paul, 56
painful emotions, 5, 7–8
Palmer, Parker, 131
Passions, The (Solomon), 23
patience, 37, 38–39
Paul, on emotions, 24, 36, 49, 70,
    77, 79, 82–83, 98–9
Philippians, Letter to the, 49
Phillips, Adam, 147
Pieper, Josef, 35, 38, 84
Pinker, Steven, 152
Plutarch, 76
pornography, 46
positive emotions, 6, 7–8
practice, of compassion, 91–92
pride, 6, 8, 26, 77–83
Proverbs, Book of, 79, 138
Psalms
    emotions in, 3, 13, 17, 55, 65,
        97–98
psychology
    of development, 65–69, 78,
        89–90
    and happiness, 60–62
    moral, 30–31
    positive, 4–5, 60–62
    and religion, 30–31

reason, and emotions, 23–25, 103,
    148–55
religion
    emotions and, 11–12, 137–45
    and hope, 41–42
    and psychology, 30–31
resurrection, 18
reverence, 8, 12, 20–22, 86
Ricoeur, Paul, 63, 113, 125, 154
romance, 73–74
Romans, Letter to the, 24, 82,
    98–99, 111–12

sadness, 38–39
Sandel, Michael, 129
Savor: Mindful Eating (Hahn and
    Cheung), 47–48
Scarry, Elaine, 16, 48
Schindler's List, 30
Schjeldahl, Peter, 151
Schweiker, William, 50–51
science, and wonder, 14–15
Secular Age, A (Taylor), 12, 63
self-compassion, 92–96
Seligman, Martin, 4–5
Shweder, Richard, 147
Siegel, Daniel, 5, 24, 62, 66, 67–68,
    89, 150
Silent Spring (Carson), 15
Simmel, Georg, 120
Snyder, C.R., 39–40
solidarity, 131–32
Solomon, 88
Solomon, Robert, 23
Sophocles, 14
Spiritual Exercises (Ignatius), 101,
    143–44
Spohn, William, 24–25, 115
Steiner, George, 16, 112, 153
Stoicism, 4, 24, 104, 109
Suchocki, Marjorie Hewitt, 124, 125
sympathy, 113

Taylor, Charles, 12, 15, 62, 63–64,
    101, 102, 152–53

temperance, 36
 and humility, 85
Teresa of Avila, 101
threat-protecting systems, 9–10
Toulmin, Stephen, 14, 102
Trible, Phyllis, 88
trust, 111

Unger, Roberto, 70, 73, 81,
 110–14

Vaillant, George, 3, 6, 28–29, 31,
 56, 125
Varieties of Religious Experience
 (James), 139–40
Veling, Terry, 128, 134
Virtues

Aquinas on, 4
 and emotions, 4, 109–17
 theological, 109–17
Virtues for Ordinary Christians
 (Keenan), 94–96
Virtuous Passions (Harak), 49
Visser, Margaret, 119, 120
vulnerability, 104–5

Wesley, John, 102
Wheelwright, Philip, 20
Woodruff, Paul, 20, 21, 86
wonder, 6–7, 12, 13–16
 and reverence, 20–21
 and science, 14–15

Yearley, Lee, 35, 36, 38, 84